1. Patricia Green
   writer-producer

2. David L. Wolper
   producer

3. Alan Shayne
   producer and former
   President, Warner Bros. TV

4. Kevin Connor
   director

ABOUT THE COVER

On the front cover are four outstanding individuals working in television today.

Writer Patricia Green has written for many television series including Eight is Enough, Scarecrow and Mrs. King, and Cagney and Lacey, for which she won an Emmy Award in 1985. In addition, she has served as story editor and executive script consultant on numerous series as well as the mini-series North and South, for which she also wrote the teleplay. Miss Green is also a producer and is currently developing series, movies of the week, and features for a major television production company,

David L. Wolper is a legendary producer whose accomplishments in the business span nearly thirty years. He has made over 500 films which have won more than 150 awards including Oscars, Emmys, Golden Globes, and the Peabody Awards.
His work as a producer spans all forms of entertainment, documentaries, feature films, television series, specials, and longforms such as movies and mini-series made for television. He was responsible for such landmark television presentations such as the 12 hour "Roots" in 1977, the 1984 Olympic Games Ceremonies, and most recently, the Statue of Liberty spectacular in New York City in 1986. Known for his historical dramas and biographies, he is currently executive producing the mini-series "Napoleon and Josephine".

Alan Shayne has led a distinguished career in television. For years, he was considered the "dean" television industry executives having served as President of Warner Bros. Television for ten years until 1986. As head of the Studio, Warner Bros. TV experienced unprecedented success in the 1970's and 80's under his administration. Currently, Mr. Shayne is now an executive producer.

Kevin Connor, an Englishman, is one of the more dynamic directors working in the industry today. He has directed movies and mini-series such as Master of the Game; Mistral's Daughter; North and South, Book II; and most recently The Lion In Africa for HBO Pictures. As a director of episodic television, he has worked on such successful series as Moonlighting; Hart to Hart; and Remington Steele.

WHO'S WHO

IN

<u>TELEVISION</u> ®

**PRODUCERS
DIRECTORS
WRITERS
THE NETWORKS
PRODUCTION COMPAMIES
TELEVISION STUDIOS
PAY/CABLE SERVICES**

FIRST EDITION - 1987

Packard House
Beverly Hills, California

Packard House Books is a Division of PACKARD COMMUNICATIONS, Inc.

Inquiries should be addressed to Packard Communications,
P.O. Box 2187, Beverly Hills, California 90213

WHO'S WHO In Television ® and WHO'S WHO In The
Motion Picture Industry ® are published annually by
Packard Communications.

Reasonable effort has been made in the accurate
compilation of information contained in the publica-
tion; the publisher, however, assumes no liability
for errors or ommissions.

Copyright © 1987 Rodman W. Gregg

ISBN 0-941710-11-4

LIBRARY OF CONGRESS CATALOG CARD NUMBER PENDING

How To Use The Book

<u>WHO'S WHO IN TELEVISION</u>   is designed for easy use. As a comprehensive business reference covering the television industry, each listing has been carefully researched in order to give the user the essential information on the individual or company that is needed.

In editing this book, we have tried to be as comprehensive as possible. For each listing in the various categories, each individual will have a contact address or business phone number. This usually can be, especially in the case of directors and writers, the individual's agent, business manager, attorney, or address of their place of business. For producers, many times they have offices at the studios in which they currently development deals or current series or productions. In many cases, we have tried to list several contacts for an individual.

Under the credits section, the order of credits shown is usually series credits first, then movies of the week (m.o.w). For simplicity's sake, the abbreviation "m.o.w." in this book is synonymous with "telefeature" and "movie made for television". Many persons listed work in both feature films and television. While the scope of this book does not cover motion pictures, we have included notations in italics to denote that an individual may also have credits in that medium, e.g. *has directed over 15 features including.....*   or *feature films include....... .* For information on persons working in film, we recommend our reference <u>*WHO'S WHO IN THE MOTION PICTURE INDUSTRY*</u>, now in it's sixth edition.

Finally, in editing this book, we may have inadvertently missed a few people who should be included within these pages. Write us and let us know and we will do our best to be more comprehensive in successive editions.

The editors welcome any comments and suggestions. Let us hear from you. And it is our wish that this volume will be of help and interest to you in whatever your pursuit in the business.

Rodman W. Gregg
Senior Editor

ACKNOWLEDGEMENTS

Preparing each edition of Who's Who requires many months of prepartaion. For making our task easier by lending their generous assistance, the publisher would like to thank the following individuals and organizations:

Glyniss Anthony and Jim Roper of the Academy of Television Arts & Sciences; Harriet Baron, Lorimar-Telepictures; Georff Brandt, A.P.A.; Michael Binkow of Fox, Inc.; Joseph Curatolo of the Writers Guild of America-West; Doug Duitsman and Barbara Tuuri, Warner Bros. Television; Will Day, Filmfair; George Faber, Viacom, Inc.; Gwen Feldman, Samuel French, Inc.; Jerry Goldberg and Elaine Leung, CBS Entertainment; Cindy Hauser, Stephen J. Cannell Productions; Ed Gradinger, Gloria Lamont, and Kim Yost, New World Television; Ed Pine, Walt Disney Co.; Kim Reed, MGM/UA; Scott Siegler, Tri-Star TV; Tom Stepanchak, Dick Clark Prods.; David Solomon, 20th Century Fox; Kimberly Wells and Al Neuman, Rogers & Cowan; and Lew Wexner, Fries Entertainment.

STAFF

RODMAN GREGG
Senior Editor

ROD PYLE
Associate Publisher

SUSAN J. AIELLO
Art Director

CHARLES EDWARDS
Photographer

GWEN FELDMAN
Publishing Consultant

ELIZABETH PATERSON
Canadian Representative

TABLE OF CONTENTS

FORWARD

This being the inaugaral edition of *WHO'S WHO IN TELEVISION,* we are hoping that this book will meet with the same success of our film industry reference book, *WHO'S WHO IN THE MOTION PICTURE INDUSTRY,* now in it's fifth edition. Most importantly, this book is meant to fill a need for those working in the television business for a comprehensive, personal guide to the industry. We have designed *Who's Who* to be a quick reference and locator to companies and individuals, along with the accompanying information that is most often needed such as credits, contact information, and position or title if with a production company, netowrk, or studio.

WHO'S WHO IN TELEVISION was originally a section of our motion picture book several years ago. But many people suggested to us that they would like to see a comprehensive guide for television in the same format. After three years, and many starts and delays, the book is now a reality. If you find it useful, by all means write to us and let us know. If you have suggestions as to content, changes, etc., we would also very much like to hear from you.

Finally, it is hoped that this guide will make your life a little easier. If you work in television, you know that this is the most competitive, difficult, and frequently frustrating business that exists, but yet we trudge on always with a new series idea, a better script, and fresh hopes that the future will bring better things.

Rodman Gregg

Important Notice

Every effort has been made to insure that the information contained in the following pages is correct. Please note: Due to the fact that television is a highly fluid business, persons working in TV are constantly moving. Some of the addresses and telephone numbers may have changed by the time you get this book. Also, directors and writers frequently change agents and this should be taken into account.

DIRECTORS

Coca-Cola **TELEVISION**

A unit of *The Coca-Cola Company*

Coca-Cola **TELECOMMUNICATIONS**

COLUMBIA/EMBASSY TELEVISION

MERV GRIFFIN
ENTERPRISES

AARON, Paul
 Agent: Creative Artists
 Office: 9100 Sunset Blvd.
 Los Angeles, CA 90069
 Tel.(213) 271-4473

credits:
m.o.w.'s: The Miracle Worker
(NBC)(Emmy Award)-1979; Thin Ice
(CBS)-1981 ;Maid In America (CBS)-
1982, When She Says No (ABC)-1984;
In Love and War (NBC)-1987; *also five
feature films*

ALLEN, Corey
 Agent: Ronnie Lief,
 Contemporary Artists
 132 Lasky Drive
 Beverly Hills, CA 90212
 Tel. (213) 278-8250

credits:
series: Spies-1987, Twilight Zone-1986;
Hill Street Blues; Paper Chase; Scare-
crow & Mrs. King; Trapper John;
Dallas; numerous pilots. m.o.w.'s:
See the Man Run; Cry Rape; Man in
the Santa Claus Suit; Yesterdays Child;
Return of Frank Cannon; Murder, She
Wrote; Brass; I-Man-1986.

ANSPAUGH, David
 Agent: William Morris Agency
 Tel. (213) 274-7451

credits:
 Series: Hill Street Blues; *feature film,
 directed Hoosiers -1986*

ANTONIO, Lou
 Agent: Lee Rosenberg,
 Triad Artists
 10100 Santa Monica Blvd.
 Los Angeles, CA 90067
 Tel.(213) 556-2727

selected credits:
series: Gentle Ben; The Flying Nun;
Partridge Family; The Rookies; Ba-
nacek; McCloud; The Steeler and the
Pittsburgh Kid; Rockford Files; Rich
Man, Poor Man (2 hours); m.o.w.'s:
Someone I Touched (ABC); Something
For Joey(CBS); The Kitty O'Neil Story
(CBS); Something So Right (CBS);
Rearview Mirror (NBC); Thirteen At
Dinner-1985; One Terrific Guy-1986.

AVERBACK, Hy
 Agent: Creative Artists
 Tel. (213) 277-4545

credits:
m.o.w.'s: She's In The Army Now; The
Girl; the Gold Watch, and Everything;
The Last Precinct-1986; *also, several
features*

AVNET, Jonathan
 (Also, see Producers)
 Business: Avnet/Kerner Co.
 505 N. Robertson Blvd.
 Los Angeles, CA 90048
 Tel. (213) 271-7408

credits:
 m.o.w.: Between Two Women (ABC)-
 1986; series: Call to Glory (ABC)-1985

directors

BADIYI, Reza
  Agent: Ronnie Lief
  Contemporary Artists
  Tel.: (213) 278-8250

credits:
m.o.w.'s: Of Mice and Men; White
Water; Blade in Hong Kong; Center-
fold Policewoman; series include:
Cagney & Lacey; Police Squad; Falcon
Crest; Mission Impossible.

BEAUMONT, Gabrielle A.
  Bus. Mgr.: Burton Merrill
  Tel.: (818) 763-6903

credits:
m.o.w.'s: The Dorthy Stratton Story;
Secrets of a Mother and Daughter;
series: Hill Street Blues; Cagney &
Lacey; M*A*S*H; Hart to Hart; Duet-
1987

BENDER, Jack
  Bus.: Sky Pictures
  11777 San Vicente # 600
  Los Angeles, CA 90049
  Agent: Triad Artists
  Tel.: (213) 556-2727

credits:
m.o.w.'s: In Love With An Older
Woman; Two Kinds of Love (CBS);
Shattered Vows (NBC); The Midnight
Hour (ABC); Letting Go (NBC); series:
Eight is Enough; Paper Chase; Fame

BINDER, Steve
  Bus.: BRB Entertaiment
  1041 N. Las Palmas Ave.
  Los Angeles, CA 90038
  Tel.: (213) 871-8102
  Agent: Lee Rosenberg, Triad
credits:
specials include: Diana Ross in Central
Park; Emmy Awards Show-1981-84;
Elvis Presley's Graceland; Ringling
Bros. and Barnum & Baily Circus-1982-
86; Father Guido Sarducci Goes to
College-1985; Pee Wee's Playhouse (co-
prod.)(CBS)-1987

BILSON, Bruce
  Bus.:Downwind Enterprised, Inc.
  12505 Sarah Street
  Studio City, CA 91604
  Agent: The Cooper Agency
  10100 Santa Monica Blvd.
  Los Angeles, CA 90067
  Tel.: (213) 277-8422

selected credits:
series: Bonanza; Bewitched; Gidget;
The Mary Tyler Moore Show;
M*A*SH; Get Smart (Emmy award);
Barney Miller; Knight Rider; Dallas;
Life With Lucy-1986; Sledge Hammer-
1986; The Colbys-1986; Spenser For
Hire-1987; m.o.w.'s: Dead Man on the
Run (ABC); The Ghosts of Buxley Hall
(NBC); The Dallas Cowboys Cheer-
leaders; The Girl Who Came Gift
Wrapped (ABC); The Love Boat
(2hr.special)-1986

BLACK, Noel
Agent: Jerry Katzman
William Morris Agency
Tel.: (213) 274-7451

credits:
I'm A Fool (PBS)-1977; The Golden
Honeymoon (PBS)-1979; m.o.w's: The
Electric Grandmother (NBC)-1981; The
Other Victim (CBS)-1981; Prime
Suspect(CBS)-1981; Happy Endings
(CBS)-1982; Quarterback Princess
(CBS)-1983; Deadly Intentions ((ABC)-
1985; Promises To Keep (CBS)-1985; A
Time to Triumph (CBS)-1986; My Two
Loves (ABC)-1986; The Doctors Wilde
(CBS)-1987.

BLECKNER, Jeffrey A.
Agent: Bauer-Benedek Agency
9255 Sunset Blvd.
Los Angeles, CA 90069
Tel.: (213)275-2421

credits:
Concealed Enemies (PBS)(Emmy
award)-1984; Do You Remember Love?
(m.o.w.)(CBS)-1985; Hill Stree Blues

BONERZ, Peter
Agent: Michael Menchell, CAA
Tel.: (213)277-4545

credits:
series: E.R.(CBS)-1985; You, Again?-
1986

BRAVERMAN, Charles
Bus.: Braverman Productions
1861 S. Bundy Dr.
Los Angeles, CA 90025
Tel.: (213) 826-6466

credits:
series: St. Elsewhere (NBC); Heart of
the City; The Wizard (CBS); What's Up
America; The Big Laff Off (Showtime);
m.o.w.'s: Prince of Bel Air; Brotherhood of Justice (ABC); specials include:
The Television Newman (Emmy
award); David Hartman-Birth and
Babies; Oscars First Fifty Years

BROWN, Georg Sanford
Agent: ICM
Tel.: (213) 550-4000

credits:
series: Lou Grant; Palmerstown;
Greatest American Hero; Fame;
Starsky and Hutch; Cagney & Lacey;
Hill Street Blues; m.o.w.'s: Roots II-
1978; Grambling's White Tiger-1981;
Miracle of the Heart-A Boys Town
Story-1986

BUTLER, Robert
Agent: Michael Rollins, ICM
Tel.: (213) 550-4000

credits include:
m.o.w's: The Blue Knight-1973; In the
Glitter Palace-1977; James Dean-
Portrait of a Friend; Dark Victory;
Concrete Beat-1985; Moonlighting-
1985; Our Family Honor-1985; Long
Time Gone-1986; Out on a Limb (mini-
series)-1987

directors

CAMPANELLA, Roy II
Agent: Geoff Brandt, A.P.A.
Tel.: (213) 273-0744

credits:
series: Knot's Landing; Knight Rider;
Hotel; Falcon Crest; Simon & Simon;
Lou Grant; Our House (NBC)-1987;
Documentary: Passion and Memory
(PBS)

CATES, Gilbert
Bus.: 195 S. Beverly Drive
Suite 414
Beverly Hills, CA 90212
Tel.: (213) 273-7773

credits:
m.o.w.'s: To All My Friends On Shore;
After The Fall; Johnny We Hardly
Knew Ye; Hobson's Choice; Burning
Rage; Consenting Adult; Child's Cry;
eries: Faerie Tale Theatre; Twilight
Zone; has directed 7 feature films
*Gilbert Cates is President of the
Directors Guild of America for 1987.*

CHAFFEY, Don
Bus.: 7020 La Presa Drive
Los Angeles, CA 90068
Tel.: (213) 851-0391
Agent: Contemporary Artists
Tel.: (213) 278-8250

credits:
series: Charlie's Angels; Vegas; T.J.
Hooker; Matt Houston; Hotel; Outlaws
(CBS)-1987; The Gift of Love (m.o.w.);
International Airport; *also four feature
films*

CHOMSKY, MARVIN J.
Agent: Len Hirshan, Wm. Morris
Tel.: (213) 274-7451

credits:
m.o.w.'s: Attica (emmy award)-1980;
The Lilac Season-1981; Evita Peron-
1981; My Body, My Child-1982; I Was
a Mail Order Bride-1982; Robert
Kennedy and His Times (CBS)-1985;
Angel In Green (CBS)-1987; mini-
series: Holocaust (Emmy award)-1978;
Inside the Third Reich (Emmy award)-
1982

COLLINS, Robert L.
Bus.: RLC Productions
760 N. La Cienega Blvd.
Los Angeles, CA 90067
Agent: Bill Haber, CAA
1888 Century Park East
Los Angeles, CA 90067
Tel.: (213) 277-4545

credits:
Gideon's Trumpet-1980; Savage
Harvest-1981; Our Family Business-
1981; Money on the Side-1981;
McGruder & Loud-1984; Mafia Prin-
cess-1985; J. Edgar Hoover-1986

COMPTON, Richard
Agent: Mark Shapiro
Shapiro-Lichtman Agency
Tel.: (213) 859-8877

credits include:
m.o.w.'s: Dead Mans Curve; Wild
Times; Barrington (CBS)-1987

14

CONNOR, Kevin G.
Agent: Elliot Webb,
Broder-Kurland-Webb
8439 Sunset Boulevard #402
Los Angeles, CA 90069
Tel.: (213) 656-9262

credits:
series: Moonlighting; Call to Glory;
Remington Steele; Hart to Hart;
m.o.w.'s: Goliath Awaits; Mistral's
Daughter, Part II; Master of the Game,
Part 1; The Return of Sherlock Holmes
(CBS)-1986; North & South, Book II
(ABC Mini-series)-1985-86; The Lion In
Africa (HBO)-1987.

COOK, Fielder
Agent: Fred Spektor, CAA
Tel.: (213) 277-4545
Atty: Morton Leavy
Leavy, Rosenswig & Hagman
11 East 44th St.
New York, NY 10017

selected credits:
Ben Casey; The 11th Hour; The Waltons; Beacon Hill; Brigadoon-1966;
The Price-1970; The Homecoming-
1971; Miles to Go Before I sleep-1975;
The Eleanor & Lou Gehrig Story-1978;
I Know Why the Caged Bird Sings-
1979; The Francis Farmer Story-1983;
Evergreen-1985; A Special Friendship-
1986; Seize the Day-1987. *also numerous feature films*

COOPER, Jackie
Agent: Ronnie Lief
Contemporary Artists
132 Lasky Drive
Beverly Hills, CA 90212
Tel.: (213) 278-8250

credits include:
series: Hennesey (also co-prod)(CBS);
the Rockford Files; Quincy; The White
Shadow; Trapper John; Cagney &
Lacey-1987; m.o.w.'s: The Last Detail-
1975; Perfect Gentlemen (also prod.)-
1977; Having Babies-1977; Rainbow;
Marathon-1979; White Mama-1979;
Leave 'em Laughing-1981; Family in
Blue-1981; Rosie (also prod.)-1982;
Glitter-1984; The Night they Saved
Christmas-1984; Izzy and Moe-1985

CRAVEN, Wes
Agent: Andrea Eastman, ICM
Tel.: (213) 550-4000
Office: Warner Bros.

credits:
m.o.w.'s: A Stranger in Our House-
1979; Invitation to Hell-1984; Chiller-
1985; Crimebusters-1985; series:
Twilight Zone (6 episodes)-1985,
*numerous features including Night-
mare on Elm Street*

CURTIS, Dan
Bus.: Dan Curtis Productions,
Inc.
9911 W. Pico Blvd.
Los Angeles, CA 90035
Tel.: (213) 577-6910

CURTIS, continued

credits:
m.o.w.'s: The Last Ride of the Dalton Gang (NBC)-1979; The Long Days of Summer (ABC)-1980; I Think I'm Having a Baby-1980; Mrs. R's Daughter-1982; The Winds of War (ABC mini-series)-1983; War And Remembrance (also producer)(30 hour mini-series for ABC).

DAMSKI, Mel
    office: Aaron Spelling Prods.
    1041 N. Formosa Avenue
    West Hollywood, CA 90046
    Agent: Dave Gersh
    Tel.: (213) 274-6611

credits: Legend of Walks Far Woman; Long Journey Back; Child Stealer-1981; American Dream-1981; For Ladies Only-1981; Badge of the Assasin-1986; Winner Never Quits-1986; Hero In The Family-1987; also several features.

DAVIDSON, Martin
    Agent: Jeff Benson
    Major Clients Agency
    1900 Avenue of the Stars
    Los Angeles, CA 90067
    Tel.: (213) 277-4998

credits:
series: Cold Steel and Neon; Family Honor; Call to Glory; m.o.w.'s: Long Gone (HBO)-1987; also 4 features

DAY, Linda
    Agent: Michael Douroux
    Lake and Douroux Agency
    Tel.: (213) 557-0700

credits:
series: Alice; Facts of Life; Different Strokes; WKRP; Who's The Boss; Bob Newhart; Dallas; St. Elsewhere; Knot's Landing

DAY, Robert
    Agent: Nicola Menchelle
    Creative Artists Agency
    Tel.: (213) 277-4545

credits include:
m.o.w.'s: Ritual of Evil; Mr. and Mrs. Bo Jo Jones; Home of Our Own; The Grass is Always Greener; Peter and Paul-1981; Running Out-1983; Cook & Perry-The Race to the Pole-1983; Hollywood Wives (mini-series)-1985; Diary of a Perfect Murder-1986; Celebration Family-1987

DONIGER, Walter
    Agent: Sam Adams/Rick Ray
    Triad Artists, Inc.
    Tel.: (213) 556-2727
    Bus.: Bettina Productions
    Tel.: (213) 659-2787

credits include:
series: Peyton Place (180 episodes); Marcus Welby; Bat Masterson; McCloud; Kung fu; m.o.w.'s: Mad Bull; Star Fall; Kentucky Woman

DUKE, Daryl
Agent: John L. Burnham
William Morris Agency
Tel.: (213) 274-7451

credits:
m.o.w.'s: I Heard the Owl Call My
Name; The Day the Lion Died; The
Thorn Birds (mini-series)(Emmy
award)-1983; *has directed 3 features*

DUBIN, Charles S.
Agent: Ron Leif
Contemporary Artists
132 Lasky Drive
Beverly Hills, CA 90212
Tel. (213) 278-8250

credits:
series: Room 222; Lou Grant; M*A*SH;
Cagney & Lacey; Starman;
m.o.w.'s: The Manions of America;
Waiting for Godot; The Gathering II;
Belle of Amherst

ELIKANN, Larry
Bus.: The Elikann Company
Tel.: (213) 470-7449
Agent: William Morris Agency
Tel.: (213) 274-7451

credits:
series: Knot's Landing; Falcon Crest;
Hill Street Blues; m.o.w.'s: The Great
Wallendas; Poison Ivy; Charlie and the
Great Balloon Race; Letter to Three
Wives; Peyton Place, The Next Genera-
tion; Dallas, The Early Years (3 hrs.);
Hands of a Stranger (NBC)-1987

ERMAN, John
Agent: Bill Haber, CAA
Tel.: (213) 277-4545

credtis include:
Letters From Three Lovers-1973;
Roots-1975; Green Eyes-1975; Roots-
The Next Generation-1978; My Old
Man-1980; Eleanor, First Lady of the
World-1981; Who Will Love My
Children (Emmy)-1983; The Atlanta
Child Murders-1984; The Two Mrs.
Grenvilles-1986; An Early Frost-1986;
When The Time Comes-1987

FALK, Harry G. Jr.
Agent: Fred Westheimer
William Morris Agency
Tel.: (213) 274-7451

credits:
Sophisticated Gents-1981; Hear No
Evil; Emerald Point NAS-1983; North
Beach and Rawhide-1985

FARGO, James
Bus.: Lions Head Productions
c/o Kaufman & Bernstein
Tel.: (213) 277-1900

credits:
Tales of the Gold Monkey-1983;
m.o.w.'s: Gus Brown & Midnight
Brewster-1985; The Last Electric
Knight-1986; *numerous features.*

FENADY, Georg J.
Agent: Shapiro-Lichtman
8827 Beverly Blvd.
Los Angeles, CA 90048
Tel.: (213) 557-2244

directors

FENADY, continued

credits:
series: Quincy (32 episodes); Simon &
Simon; The Fall Guy; T.J. Hooker; Air
Wolf; *plus six movies for television.*

FORBES, Bryan
Bus.: Pinewood Studios
Iver Heath
Bucks, England
Agent: The Agency
Tel.: (213) 277-7779

credits:
The Slipper and the Rose; Goodbye,
Norma jean; Chandlertown; Whistle
Down the Wind; *also numerous
features.*

FRIEDKIN, William
Agent: Jeff Berg, ICM
Tel.: (213)-550-4205

Credits: C.A.T. Squad (NBC)(m.o.w.)-
1986, *numerous features including*
The French Connection

GETHERS, Steven
Agent: Rowland Perkins, CAA
Tel.: (213) 277-4545

credits include:
m.o.w.'s: Jacqueline Bouvier Kennedy;
Confessions of a Married Man; Jenny's
War (4hrs.); Mercy or Murder ? (NBC)-
1987

GLASER, Paul-Michael
Agent: Andrea Eastman, ICM
Tel.: (213) 550-4000

credits:
numerous series episodes; *features:*
Band of the Hand-1986; Running Man-
1987

GOLDSTONE, James
c/o Jess Morgan
Tel.: (213) 651-1601
Agent: The Gersh Agency
Tel.: (213) 274-6611

credits:
Star Trek; Ironside; m.o.w.'s; A Clear
and Present Danger-1971; Kent State
(Emmy award)-1981, Charles & Diana-
A Royal Love Story-1981; Rita
Hayworth; Calamity Jane; The Sun
Also Rises (mini-series)-1984; *numer-*
ous features

GRAHAM, William
Agent: Fred Specktor
Creative Artists Agency
Tel.: (213) 277-4545

credits:
The Guyana Tragedy; Raid; Deadly
Encounter; Mothers Against Drunk
Drivers; Women of San Quentin;
Calendar Girl Murder; Secrets of a
Married Man-1985; Mussolini-The
Untold Story (m.o.w.)-1986; Police
Story: The Freeway Killings (m.o.w.)-
1987

GRANT, Lee
 Agent: William Morris Agency
 Tel.: (213) 274-7451

credits:
Women of Willmar-1982, When
Women Kill-1983; A Matter of Sex-
1984; Down and Out In America
(HBO)-1985; Nobody's Child-1986

GREEN, Guy M.
 Bus.: 102 Old Church Street
 London S.W. 3., England
 Agent: The Gersh Agency
 222 N. Canon Drive
 Beverly Hills, CA 90212
 Tel.: (213) 274-6611

credits:
Dr. Meg Laurel; Jimmy B. and Andre;
Inmates: A Love Story; Isabel's Choice;
The Devil's Advocate; Strong Medicine
(OPT)-1985; *also numerous features*

GREENE, David
 Agent: Creative Artists Agency
 Tel.: (213) 277-4545

credits include:
 Rich Man, Poor Man-1976; Roots-1977;
Friendly Fire; Trial of Lee Harvey
Oswald; The Guardian-1984 ;Fatal
Vision-1984; Miles to Go-1986; Circle
of Violence-1986

GREENWALD, Robert
 Bus.: Robert Greenwald
 Productions
 10510 Culver Blvd.
 Culver City, CA 90232
 Tel.: (213) 204-0404

credits:
Sharon: Portrait of a Mistress-1977;
Centerfold-1978; In the Custody of
Strangers-1982; The Burnig Bed (NBC)-
1984; Shattered Spirits-1986; On Fire-
1986; Daddy (ABC)-1987

HAINES, Randa
 Agent: Bill Bloch, ICM
 Tel.: (213) 550-4218

credits:
Under The Sky (PBS)-1979; The Jilting
of Granny Weatherall (PBS)-1980; Hill
Streeet Blues-1981-82; Alfred Hitch-
cock Presents; Just Pals (ABC)-1982;
Something About Amelia (ABC
m.o.w.)-1983; *feature: Children of a
Lesser God-1986*

HALE, Billy
 Agent: William Morris Agency
 Tel.: (213) 274-7451

credits:
m.o.w.'s: Great Nigara; Red Alert;
Caroline, Wild Child; Nightmare; How
I Spent My Summer Vacation; Mini-
series: Murder In Texas-1981, One
Shoe Makes It Murder-1982; Lace
(mini-series)-1984; Lace II-1985;
Harem-1986

HANSON, Curtus
 Agent: Leading Artists
 445 N. Bedford Drive,
 Penthouse
 Beverly Hills, CA 90210
 Tel.: (213) 858-1999

HANSON, continued

credits:
Billy's Army (ABC)-1982; The Children of Times Square (m.o.w.), *also 3 features including The Bedroom Window-1987*

HARRINGTON, Curtis
  Agent: Robert Goldfarb
  Sy Fischer Company Agency
  Tel.: (213) 969-2900

credits:
series: Hotel; Dynasty; Twilight Zone-1986; m.o.w.'s: The Cat Creature; How Awful About Alan; Killer Bees; Devil Dog-1978

HARRIS, Harry
  Agent: Jack Dytman, ICM
  Tel.: (213) 550-4000

credits:
series: Eight is Enough (40 episodes)-1977-81; Walton's; Fame (Emmy award)-1982; ABC Afternoon Special; m.o.w.: Rivkin: Bounty Hunter-1981; A Day for Thanks on Walton's Mountain-1982; Alice In Wonderland-1985; Eight is Enough: Reunion (NBC)-1987

HART, Harvey
  Bus.: Rohar Productions, Ltd.
  Toronto, Canada
  Tel.: (416) 960-2351
  Agent: Contemporary Artists
  Tel.: (213) 278-8250
credits:
m.o.w.'s: Maserati and the Brain-1982; Born Beautiful-1982; Master of the Game (co-directed)-1984; Reckless

Disregard-1982; Beverly Hills Madam-1986; Stone Fox (NBC)-1987

HECKERLING, Amy
  Agent: David Gersh
  The Gersh Agency
  Tel.: (213) 274-6611

credits:
Twilight Zone-1986; The Sweet Smell of Success (CBS)-1987; *3 features including Fast Times at Ridgemont High.*

HEFFRON, Richard
  Agent: Fred Specktor, CAA
  Tel.: (213) 277-4545

credits:
The California Kid; The Morning After; I Will Fight No More Forever; Young Joe Kennedy; A Rumor of War-1981; A Whale for the Killing-1981;The Mystic Warrior-1984; V-The Final Battle-1984; North and South (ABC Mini-series)-1985; Samaritan-1986; The Lenell Geter Story-1986; *also directed 7 features*

HICKOX, Douglas
  Agent: Shapiro-Lichtman
  Tel.: (213) 859-8877

credits:
m.o.w.'s: The Hound of the Baskervilles; The Master of Ballantrae; Blackout; mini-series: Mistral's Daughter-1985; Sins-1986

HOLCOMB, Rod
Agent: Broder-Kurland-Webb
8439 Sunset Blvd.
Los Angles, CA 90069
Tel.: (213)656-9262

credits:
series: The Greatest American Heroe;
The A-Team; Scarecrow and Mrs.
King; The Equalizer; Spies; m.o.w.'s:
No Man's Land; Two Fathers; The
Cartier Affair; The Chase; Blind Justice;
Stillwatch.

HUGHES, Terry
Agent: William Morris Agency
Tel. (213) 274-7451

credits:
series: Report to Murphy; Square Pegs;
Empire;
m.o.w.'s: Sunset Limosene (CBS); For
Love or Money (CBS)

HUSSEIN, Waris
Agent:Elliott Webb
Broder, Kurland & Webb
8439 Sunset Blvd., Ste 402
Los Angeles, CA 90069
Tel. (213) 656-9262

credits:
Edward and Mrs. Simpson; Death
Penalty (NBC); And Baby Makes Six
(NBC); Callie and Son (CBS); Coming
Out of the Ice (CBS): Little
Gloria...Happy At Last (NBC); Princess
Daisy (NBC); Winter of Our Discontent
(CBS); Arch Of Triumph (CBS);
Copacabana (CBS); Surviving (ABC);
When the Bough Breaks (NBC)

IRVING, Richard
(also, see Producers)
Agent: Stephanie Rogers & Assoc.
3855 Lankershim Blvd. # 218
North Hollywood, CA 91604
Tel.: (818) 509-1010

credits include:
series: The Insiders; Airwolf, Chips;
m.o.w.s: The Virginian (created & dir.);
Cyborg; Prescription Murder; Break-
out; Class of '65; mini-series: Seventh
Avenue (6hrs.)-1977; The Jesse Owens
Story (4hrs.)-1984.

JAMESON, Jerry
Agent: William Morris Agency
Tel.: (213) 274-7451

credits:
m.o.w.'s: Heatwave-1974; The Deadly
Tower-1975; The Call fo the Wild-1976;
A Fire In The Sky-1978; Ther Return of
Will Kane-1980; Hotline-1982; Starflight: The Plane That Couldn't Land-
1983; Cowboy-1983; This Girl for Hire-
1983; The Cowboy and the Ballerina-
1984; Stormin' Home-1985; Police
Plaza (CBS)-1986

JOHNSON, Lamont
Agent: Geoff Brandt, A.P.A.
9000 Sunset Blvd.
Los Angeles, CA 90069
Tel.: (213) 273-0744

credits include:
m.o.w.'s: My Sweet Charlie; The
Execution of Private Slovik; Escape
From Iran; Crisis at Central High;
Unnatural Causes (m.o.w.)-1986;
numerous features

21

directors

JORDAN, Glenn
  Bus.: 9401 Wilshire Blvd.,Ste.700
  Beverly Hills, CA 90212
  Tel.:(213)278-7700

credits:
m.o.w's: Eccentricities of a Nightengale
(PBS); In the Matter of Karen Ann
Quinlan; Sunshine Christmas; Ben-
jamin Franklin (Emmy award); The
Women's Room; Heartsonds;
Toughlove; Dress Gray; Promise
(Hallmark Hall of Fame)-1987; *also, 3
feature films*

KAGAN, Jeremy Paul
  Agent: Triad Artists
  Bus.: 11812 San Vicente Blvd.
  Suite 200
  Los Angeles, CA 90049
  Tel.: (213) 826-0909

credits:
m.o.w.'s: Katherine; My Dad Lives in a
Downtown Hotel; Courage; Unwed
Father; Judge Dee; *has directed 6
feature films.*

KORTY, John
  Agent: Bob Wunch
  Tel.: (213) 278-1955
  Bus.: Korty Films
  200 Miller Avenue
  Mill Valley, CA 94941

credits include:
m.o.w.'s: The People-1972; The Autobiography of Miss jane Pittman-1974;
Who are the Debolts-1978; A Christmas Without Snow-1980; The Haunting Passion-1983; Second Sight-A Love
Story-1984; The Ewok Adventure-1985;
A Deadly Business; Resting Place-1986

KULIK, Buzz
  Agent: Hal Ross
  William Morris Agency
  Tel.: (213) 859-4324

credits:
 Rage of Angels-1983; George Washington (mini-series)-1984; Kane & Abel
(mini-series)-1985; Women of Valor-
1986; Her Secret Life-1987

LANG, Rocky
  Agent: David Lonner, ICM
  Tel.: (213) 550-4000
credits:
The Great One-A Tribute to Jackie
Gleason; The Making of Tootsie;
Remington Steele (NBC)

LANGTON, Simon
  c/o Peter Murphy
  162-168 Regent Street
  London, England W1R, 5TA
  Tel.: (01) 437-9700

credits:
m.o.w.'s: Anna Karenina (CBS)-1985;
The Lost Honor of Katherine Beck
(CBS); Smiley's People (BBC); Rebecca

LEE, Joanna
Agent: The Agency
10351 Santa Monica Blvd.
Los Angeles, CA 90025
Tel.: (213)551-3000

credits:
Mirror, Mirror-1979; Children of
Divorce-1980

LEWIS, Robert M.
Agent: Bob Wunch
Tel.: (213) 278-1955

credits:
m.o.w.'s: The Miracle of Kathy Miller;
Ther Sam Sheppard Murder Case; A
Private Battle; Fallen Angel; The Raid
on Short Creek; Agatha Cristie's
Sparkling Cyanide; Flight 90: Disaster
on the Potomac; Lost in London; A
Stranger Waits; Embassy
LONDON, Jerry
Agent: Creative Artists
Tel.: (213) 277-4545

credits include:
m.o.w.'s: Father Figure; Bill CArnery;
Gift of Life; Swan Song; mini-series:
Shogun-1980; Ellis Island; The Scarlet
and the Black-1983; Chiefs-1983; series
include: Mary Tyler Moore; Bob
Newhart; Rockford Files; Hotel;
Chicago Story-1986

LOWRY, Dick
Bus.: Lowry Productions
Tel.: (213) 653-6115
Agent: Geoff Brandt, A.P.A.
9000 Sunset Blvd.
Los Angeles, CA 90069

Tel.: (213) 273-0744
credits:
m.o.w.s: Ohms-1979; The Gambler
(CBS)-1979; Jayne Mansfield (CBS)-
1979; Angel Dusted (NBC)-1981;
Coward of the County (1981); A Few
Days in Weasal Creek (cbs)-1981;
Rascals and Robbers (CBS)-1982;
Missing Children; A Mother's Story-
1982; Living Proof-1982; Gambler II-
1983; Wet Gold (ABC)-1984; Murder
With Mirrors (CBS)-1985; The Tough-
est Man In The World-1985; Wild
Horses-1985; American Harvest-1986;
The Gambler III-1987; Mini-series:
Dream West (7 hrs.)-1986

LYNCH, Paul
Agent: Barry Perelman Agency
9200 Sunset Blvd.. Suite 531
Los Angeles, CA 90069
Tel.: (213) 274-5999
credits:
series: Voyagers; Blacke's Magic;
Murder, She Wrote; Twilight Zone;
Moonlighting; Cameo By Night (NBC)-
1987

MALONE, Nancy
Agent: Irv Schecter Co.
9300 Wilshire Blvd.
Beverly Hills., CA 90212
Tel.: (213) 278-8070

credits:
series: Dynasty; Hotel; Starman,
Cagney & Lacey; There Were Times,
Dear (PBS)-1986

MANN, Daniel
Mgr: Berke Management Co.
15910 Ventura Blvd.
Encino, CA 91436

credits:
Playing for Time-1980; The Day the
Loving Stopped-1981; *has directed 20
feature films*

MANN, Delbert
Agent: William Morris Agency
Tel.: (213) 274-7451

credits include:
m.o.w.'s: The Man Without A Coun-
try; Tell Me My Name; Breaking Up;
All Quiet On The Western Front; To
Find My Son; Member of the Wedding;
The Gift of Love; Love Leads the Way;
The Last Days of Patton-1986; April
Morning (CBS)-1987; *also, has directed
over 20 feature films.*

MANN, Michael
(Also, see Producers)
office: Universal Studios
Tel.: (818) 777-1112

credits:
m.o.w.: The Jericho Mile; *features
include The Keep; Thief; Manhunter-
1986*

MARGOLIN, Stuart
Agent: Lou Pitt; ICM
Tel.: (213) 550-4321

credits:
m.o.w.'s: Suddenly Love-1979' The
Long Summer of George Adams-1981;

A Shining Season-1981; Bret Maverick-
1981; The Glitter Dome (HBO)-1983

MARKOWITZ, Robert
Agent: John Ptak
William Morris Agency
Tel.: (213) 274-7451

credits:
m.o.w.'s: Children of the Night (CBS);
Phantom of the Opera (CBS); The
Deadliest Season (CBS); Song of Myself
(CBS); My Mother's Secret Life (ABC);
Pray TV (ABC); Along Way Home
(ABC); Alex, the Life a Child (ABC);
Adam II, the Song Continues (NBC);
Life or Death in the Emergency Room
(HBO), special: The Wall (ABC)

MAYBERRY, Russ
Agent: Herb Tobias & Assoc.
1901 Aveneu of the Stars,#840
Los Angeles, CA 90067
credits:
m.o.w.'s: The $5.20 Dream; Reunion;
Matter of Life and Death; Million
Dollar Deliverance; Young Runaways;
The Rebels; Challenge of a Lifetime; A
Place To Call Home-1987; numerous
series episodes.

McLAGLEN, Andrew V.
Bus.: P.O. Box 1056
Friday Harbor, Wash. 98250
Tel.: (206)-378-4990

credits:
m.o.w.'s: The Shadow Riders (CBS)-
1982; The Dirty Dozen-the Next
Mission-1985; mini-series: The Blue
and the Gray (CBS)-1982; On Wings of

Eagles (NBC)-1986; *has directed 20 feature films.*

MEDAK, Peter
  Agent: William Morris Agency
  Tel.: (213) 274-7451

credits:
Third Girl From the Left; The Baby Sittter; Mistress of Paradise; Cry For The Strangers; *also 7 feature films.*

METZGER, Alan
  Agent: Sam Adams, Triad Artists
  Tel.: (213) 556-2727

credits include: The Equalizer (CBS)-1987; m.o.w.'s: Kojak: The Price of Justice

MILLER, Sharon
  Agent: Geoff Brandt, A.P.A.
  9000 Sunset Blvd.
  Los Angeles, CA 90069
  Tel.: (213) 273-0744

credits:
series: In Search Of..; Paper Chase (Showtime); The Woman Who Willed A Miracle (ABC)(Emmy Award); Cagney & Lacey-1984-86; Cagney & Lacey (2 hr. episode)-1987; L.A. Law (NBC)-1986; Kay O'Brien-1986; m.o.w.: Pleasures (ABC)

MOXEY, John Llewellyn
  Agent: Jeff Cooper,
  Cooper Agency
  1900 Avenue of the Stars
  Los Angeles, CA 90067
  Tel.: (213) 277-8422

credits:
m.o.w.'s: The Night Stalker; Intimate Strangers; No Place to Hide; The Violation of Sarah McDavid; Through Naked Eyes; Sadie and Son (CBS)-1987; series: Murder, She Wrote; Magnum P.I.; Miami Vice; Matlock

O'HARA, Terrence
  Bus.: 13719 Ventura Blvd.
  Suite H
  Sherman Oaks, CA 91423
  Tel.: (818) 906-3439
  messages: (213) 467-4067

credits:
Ghostwriter-1985; Indian Summer-1985; Undercover-1987

PASETTA, Marty
  Office: 8322 Beverly Blvd.#205
  Los Angeles, CA 90048
  Tel.: (213) 655-8500

credits:
 Live and in Person (NBC); Sinatra Ol' Blue Eyes (ABC); The Grammy Awards (8 years); The Emmy Awards (2 years); AFI Salutes (8 years); The Academy Awards (15 years).

PATCHETT, Tom
  (Also, see Prod's. & Writers)
  Bus. Mgr.: Bernie Brillstein
  Tel.: (213) 275-6135

credits:
Washingtoon (also prod.)(Showtime)-1985

PEERCE, Larry
  Agent: Geoff Brandt, A.P.A.
  Tel. (213) 273-0744

credits:
A Stranger Who Looks Like Me-1974; I
Take These Men; Love Lives On-1985;
The Fifth Missle-1986; A Prison For
Children-1986; Queenie (ABC mini-
series)-1987

PETRIE, Daniel M.
  Bus. Mgr.: Donner, Schrier & Zucker
  15233 Ventura Blvd., Suite 1100
  Sherman Oaks, CA 91403
  Tel.: (818) 981-5584

credits:
m.o.w.'s: Silent Night, Lonely Night-
1969; Eleanor and Franklin-1976;
Harry S. Truman-Plain Speaking
(PBS)-1976; Sybil-1977; Eleanor & and
Franklin: The White House Years; The
Quinns-1977; The Dollmaker-1984; The
Execution of Raymond Graham-1985;
Half a Lifetime; *numerous features.*

PHILIPS, Lee
  Agent: Martin Shapiro
  Shapiro-Lichtman Agency
  Tel.: (213) 859-8877

credits:
Valentine; The Girl Most Likely to...;
The War Between the Tates: Sweet
Hostage; Mae West; Space (CBS mini-
series)-1985; Barnum (CBS)-1986

PINTOFF, Ernest
  Agent: Contemporary Artists
  132 Lasky Drive
  Beverly Hills, CA 90212
  Tel.: (213) 278-8250

credits:
series: White Shadow; Dallas; Knots
Landing; Falcon Crest; Call to Glory;
m.o.w.: Human Feelings; *also seven
features*

PRESSMAN, Michael
  Agent: Rick Nicita, CAA
  Tel.: (213) 277-4545

credits:
m.o.w.'s: Like Mom, Like Me; The
Imposter; Secret Passions (NBC)-1987;
special: And the Children Shall Lead
(PBS)

RICH, John
  (Also, see Producers)
  Bus.Mgr.: FKB
  Tel.: (213) 277-0700

credits:
series: Mr. Sunshine-1986

ROSENFELT, Joan
  office: 204 West 10th Street
  New York City, NY 10014

credits:
Blackout on Honeysuckle Lane (PBS)-
1987

WARNER BROS. TELEVISION
A Warner Communications Company

directors

ROTH, Bobby
Office: 7469 Melrose Ave., Suite 35
Los Angeles, CA 90046
Tel.: (213) 651-0288
Agent: Triad Artists
Tel.: (213) 556-2727

credits:
Miami Vice; The Insiders; The Man
Who Fell to Earth; m.o.w.: Tonight's
The Night (ABC)-1987; Baja Oklahoma
(HBO)-1987; *features include Boss's
Son, Heartbreakers*

SANDRICH, Jay
Agent: Ron Meyer, CAA
Tel.: (213)277-4545
Office: GTG Entertainment
Tel.: (213) 836-5537

selected credits:
Mary Tyler Moore Show (2 Emmy
awards)-1970-77; Bob Newhart Show;
Soap-1977-78; The Golden Girls; The
Cosby Show-1984-87

SARGENT, Joseph
Agent: Shapiro-Lichtman
8827 Beverly Blvd.
Los Angeles, CA 90048
Tel.: (213) 859-8877

credits include:
m.o.w.'s: Tribes-1969; The Marcus
Nelson Murders (Emmy award)-1973;
Friendly Persuasion-1975; Amber
Waves-1980; Terrible Joe Moran-1982;
Passion Flower; Space (mini-series)-
1984; Love is Never Silent; Of Pure
Blood; There Must Be A Pony-1986;
*features include Jaws-The   Revenge -
1987*

SCHAEFER, George
Business: Schaefer/Karpf
  Productions
3500 W. Olive Blvd., Suite 730
Burbank, CA 91505
Tel. (818) 953-7770
Agent: Rowland Perkins
Creative Artists Agency

credits include:
m.o.w.'s: Victoria Regina; Magnificent
Yankee; Little Moon of Alban; First
You Cry; A War of Children; Our
Town; Blind Ambition; The Bunker; A
Piano For Mrs. Cimino; The Booth;
Children In the Crossfire; Stone Pillow-
1985; Mrs. Delafield Wants to Marry-
1985

SCHLONDORFF, Volker
Agent: Gary Salt
Paul Kohner Agency
Tel.: (213) 550-1060

credits:
m.o.w.'s: Death of a Salesman; A
Gathering of Old Men -1987; *numerous
features*

SCOTT, Oz
Agent: Jeff Cooper
The Cooper Agency
10100 Santa Monica Blvd.
Los Angeles, CA 90067
Tel.: (213) 277-8422
messages : (818) 761-7100

credits:
series: The Jeffersons; Alcie; Gimme a
Break; Archie Bunker's Place; Hill
Street Blues; 227, *also, 2 features.*

SHEARER, Harry
c/o KCRW-FM
Tel.: (213) 450-5183

credits:
Martin Mull's History of White People
(HBO)-1986

SPOTTISWOODE, Roger
Agent: Bill Bloch, ICM
Tel.: (213) 550-4000

credits:
The Last Innocent Man (HBO)-1986;
also 4 features

STERN, Steven H.
Agent: Broder-Kurland-Webb
8439 Sunset Blvd., Ste. 402
Los Angeles, CA 90069
Tel.: (213)656-9262

credits:
m.o.w.'s: Getting Married; The Ghost
of Flight 40; Miracle on Ice; A Small
Killing; Forbidden Love; Baby Sister;
Many Happy Returns; This Park is
Mine (HBO)-1985; Draw-1986; Run-
ning-1986

STORM, Howard
Agent: Robinson, Weintraub, Gross
8424 Melrose Place, Suite C
Los Angeles, CA 90069
Tel.: (213)653-5802

credits:
series: Rhoda; Laverne & Shirley; Mork
& Mindy; Taxi; Gimme a Break; Prime
Times (NBC special), Faerie Tale
Theatre (Showtime)

SWEENEY, Bob
Agent: The Cooper Agency
10100 Santa Monica Blvd.
Los Angeles, CA 90067
Tel.: (213) 277-8422

credits:
m.o.w.'s: Return to Mayberry-1986; My
Father, My Son-1987; series: Crazy
Like a Fox; Dynasty; Trapper John;
Scarecrow and Mrs. King

SZWARC, Jeannot
Bus.: Terpsichore Productions
10100 Santa Monica Blvd.
Los Angeles, CA 90067
Tel.: (213) 553-8200

credits include:
Night of Terror-1972; You'll Never See
Me Again-1973; The Small Miracle-
1973; Crime Club-1975; The Murder in
the Rue Morgue-1987; *also 7 features*

TAHSE, Martin
(also, see Producers)
Bus.: Martin Tahse Productions
323 Veteran Avenue
Los Angeles, CA 90024
Tel. (213) 476-7435

credits:
Salems's Children-1987

TAYLOR, Don
Agent: The Gersh Agency
Tel.: (213) 274-6611

credits:
m.o.w.'s: Circle of Children; Broken
Promises; Red Flag; Drop Out Father;
September Gun; My Wicked, Wicked

directors

TAYLOR, continued

Ways; Classified Cove; Ghost of a
Chance-1987.

TAYLOR, Jud
  Agent: Creative Artists Agency
  Tel.: (213) 277-4545

credits:
m.o.w.'s: Tail Gunner Joe; Mary White;
The Last Tennant; A Question of
Honor; License to Kill; Out of Dark-
ness; Broken Vows; Foxfire (CBS)-1987

VOGEL, Virgil
  Agent: David Shapira & Associates
  Tel.: (818) 906-0322

credits:
series: Magnum P.I.; Knight Rider;
Spenser for Hire-1987; mini-series:
Centenial-1979; Beulah Land-1980;
m.o.w.'s: Law of the Land-1976;
Today's F.B.I.-1981; Street Hawk-1985;
Condor-1986

WEILL, Claudia
  Agent: Joan Hyler
  William Morris Agency
  Tel.: (213) 274-7451

credits:
The Other Half of the Sky; The Great
Love Experiement (Emmy); Johnny
Bull-1986, Twilight Zone; Fast Times at
Ridgemont High; *2 features*

WENDKOS, Paul
  Agent: Creative Artists
  Tel.: (213)-277-4545
credits:
m.o.w.'s: Fear No Evil-1969; The
Brotherhood of the Bell-1970; A Death
of Innocence-1971; The Underground
Man-1974; The Legend of Lizzie
Borden-1975; The Death of Richie-1977;
79 Park Avenue-1979; The Ordeal of
Dr. Mudd-1980; The Five of Me-1981;
Cocaine: One Man's Poison-1983; The
Execution-1985; Picking Up The
Pieces-1985; Sister Margaret and the
Saturday Nifgt Ladies-1986, Rage of
Angels: The Story Continues (mini-
series)-1986; Right to Die-1987; *also,
numerous features.*

WERNER, Peter
  Agent: The Gersh Agency
  Tel.: (213) 274-6611

Credits:
m.o.w.'s: Battered; Aunt Mary; Hard
Knox; I Married A Centerfold; LBJ-
The Early Years -1987; series: Family;
Hometown; Moonlighting
(8 episodes)-1985-86; Call to Glory;
short film: In the Region of Ice (A.F.I.)
(Academy Award); *also, 2 features*

WIARD, William O.
 Agent: Triad Artists
 Tel.: (213) 556-2727

credits:
m.o.w.'s: Scott Free-1976; The Girl, the
Gold Watch, and Everything-1980; Ski
Lift to Death-1982; This House Pos-
sessed-1981; Help Wanted: Male-1982;
Fantasies-1982; Deadly Lessons-1983;
Kicks-1985; *feature: Tom Horn*

WRYE, Donald
 Agent: John Ptak
 William Morris Agency
 Tel.: (213) 274-7451

credits include:
Born Innocent-1974; The Entertainer-
1977; Fire On The Mountain-1982;
Divorce Wars: A Love Story; Heart of
Steel-1983; Amerika (16 hour ABC
mini-series)-1987

ZINBERG, Michael
 (Also, See Producers)
 Agent: Broder-Kurland-Webb
 Bus.: American Flyer Films
 Tel.: (213) 277-2211

credits include:
Mary Tyler Moore Show; Duet (FBC);
Mr. Belvedere (ABC); Heart of the City
(ABC)-1987; L.A. Law (NBC)-1987

ZWICK, Ed
 Agent: ICM
 Tel.: (213) 550-4205
 Bus. Bedford Falls Productions
 Tel: (818) 760-5000

credits:
series: Family (ABC); The Best of
Times (NBC)-1986; The Insiders; Thirty
Something (ABC)-1987; m.o.w.'s:
Paper Dolls (ABC)-1982; Having It All
(ABC)-1982; Special Bulletin (NBC
Dramatic Special)(emmy award)-1983

PRODUCERS

producers

ABATEMARCO, Frank
(Also, see Writers)
Agent: Leading Artists
Tel.: (213) 858-1999

credits:
Micky Spillane's Mike Hammer-1983-
84; Like Father, Like Daughter (CBS
m.o.w.)-1985

ABDO, Nick
Agent: David Shapira & Associates
15301 Ventura Blvd. # 345
Sherman Oaks, CA 91423
Tel.: (818) 906-9845

credits:
series: Happy Days Anniversary
Special-1976; Blansky's Beauties-1977;
Laverne & Shirley-1978-79; Brothers &
Sisters-1978-79; Working Stiffs-1979-80;
m.o.w.: Still the Beaver (CBS)-1983

ABRAHMS, Gerald W.
Bus.: Phoenix Entertainment
310 San Vicente Blvd.,Ste.300
Los Angeles, CA 90048
(213) 657-7502

credits include:
m.o.w.'s: The Defection of Simas
Kudirka; James Dean-Portrait of a
Friend; Having Babies I, II, and III; Red
Alert; Ski Lift to Death; Letters From
Frank; Marian Rose White-1983; Found
Money-1983; Scorned and Swindled-
1984; Florence Nightingale-1985;
Thompson's Last Run-1986; Monte
Carlo (mini-series)-1986; *Hearts of Fire
(feature)-1986*

ADELSON, Gary
Office: Lorimar-Telepictures
3970 Overland Blvd.
Culver City, CA 90230
Tel.: (213) 202-4242

credits:
series: Eight is Enough; Courthouse
Detective; Spies-1987; m.o.w.'s: Sybil;
The Winter of Our Discontent (Co-
prod. with Malcolm Stuart) (CBS)-
1985; Lace; Lace-part II; *features
include The Boy Who Could Fly & In
the Mood.*

ALLEN, Irwin
Bus.: Columbia Pictures Industries
The Burbank Studios
Prod. 5, Room 101
Burbank, CA 91505
Tel.: (818) 954-3601
Agent: Jerry Katzman,
William Morris Agency

credits:
series: as creator/producer: Voyage to
the Bottom of the Sea; Lost in Space;
Land of the Giants; The Time Tunnel;
Swiss Family Robinson; Code Red;
m.o.w.'s: Adventures of the Queen;
Flood; Fire; Hanging by a Thread;
Cave-in; Memory of Eva Ryker; The
Night the Bridge Fell Down; mini-
series: The Return of Captain Nemo;
Alice in Wonderland; *numerous
features including The Towering
Inferno*

ALLYN, William
Bus.: McNeil/Allyn Films
12031 Ventura Blvd. #3
Studio City, CA 91604
Tel.: (818) 763-30771

credits:
m.o.w.'s: The Last Child-1971; And No
One Could Save Her; Once Upon A
Time Is Now-1978; The Story of
Princess Grace-1978; Echoes of the
Sixties-1979; Kenya (mini-series)-1987;
Berlin Stories (mini-series)-1988;
features include Rich and Famous

ANDRE, Blue
Bus.: Blue Andre Productions
Reeves Entertainment Group
3500 W. Olive Avenue, Ste 500
Burbank, CA 91505
Tel.: (818) 953-7617

credits:
m.o.w.'s: Rape & Marriage: The
Rideout Case (co-produced with
Vanessa Greene)-1980; Wait Till Your
Mother Gets Home (NBC)-1983;
Hobson's Choice (CBS)-1983; A Time
To Live (NBC)-1985; Unnatural Causes
(CBS)-1987

ANDREWS, Ralph
Bus.: Ralph Andrews Productions
Columbia Plaza
Burbank, CA 91505
Tel.: (818) 954-4262

credits:
Liar's Club; Celebrity Sweepstakes;
You Don't Say; Lingo-1987

ARNOLD, Danny
Business: Four D Productions
9200 Sunset Blvd. # 920
Los Angeles, CA 90069
Tel.: (213) 550-7022

credits:
series: My World and Welcome To It
(Emmy)-1970; The Real McCoys,
Bewitched, That Girl, Barney Miller
(Emmy)-1982, Joe Bash-1986.

AVNET, Jon
Bus.: Avnet/Kerner Co.
505 N. Robertson Blvd.
Los Angeles, CA 90048
Tel.: (213) 271-7408

credits:
m.o.w.'s: No Other Love-1979; Home-
ward Bound; Prime Suspect-1982;
Something So Right (CBS)-1982; The
Burning Bed-1984; Silence of the Heart-
1984; Call to Glory-1984; Betwen Two
Women (also dir.)-1985; In Love & War
(with Steve Tisch)-1987; *Less Than
Zero (feature with Jordan Kerner)-1987*

BAER, Donald A.
Agent: Mark Lichtman
8827 Beverly Blvd.
Los Angeles, CA 90048
Tel.: (213) 859-8877

credits:
m.o.w.'s: Fighting Back-1979; The Boy
Who Drank Too Much-1979;
Tomorrow's Child-1981; series: Tales
of the Gold Monkey-1982; Blue Thun-
der-1984

producers

BANTA, Gloria
(also, see Writers)
Bus.: LCA/Highgate Films
16 W. 61st Street
New York, NY 10023
Tel. (212) 307-0202

credits:
Angie-1980; It's A Living -1980-81;
former V.P. comedy development for
Paramount TV. Currently writer-
producer developing half hour sitcoms
and series for Highgate.

BAYNES, Andrea
Bus.: Andrea Baynes Productions
Lorimar-Telpictures
3970 Overland Avenue
Prods. Bldg. Room 125
Culver City, CA 90230
Tel.: (213) 202-4207

credits:
m.o.w.'s as executive producer: Kate's
Secret (NBC)-1986; The Long Journey
Home (CBS)-1987. *Former Sr. Vice*
President, 20th Century Fox Television

BELL, Dave
Bus.: Dave Bell & Assoc.'s
3211 Cahuenga Blvd. West
Los Angeles, CA 90068
Tel.: (213) 851-7801

credits include:
m.o.w.'s: Nadia-1984; Do You Remember Love (NBC)-1985; specials; Shoot/
Don't Shoot-1982; Going Straight-1983;
Rich, Thin and Beautiful-1984;
Missing....Have You Seen This Person?-1985; Getting Even: Victims Fight

Back (HBO)-1984; Murder or Mercy
(HBO)-1987; Unsolved Mysteries (co-
prod.) (NBC)-1987; Alive & Well (USA
Net.)-1980-87

BELLISARIO, Donald
Bus.: Bellisarius Productions
12001 Ventura Place
Studio City, CA 91604
Tel.: (818) 763-0069

credits:
Battlestar Galactica-1980; Tales of the
Gold Monkey-1982-83; Magnum P.I.
(exec. producer)-1881-87

BENSON, Hugh

credits:
m.o.w.'s: Goliath Awaits-1981; The
Blue and the Gray-1982; The Shadow
Riders-1982; Anna Karenina (CBS)-
1985; series: Hart to Hart (ABC)

BERG, Dick
Business: Stonehenge Productions
Paramount Pictures
5555 Melrose Avenue
Los Angeles, CA 90038
Tel.: (213) 468-5000

credits:
as executive producer: m.o.w's: The
Word; Rape and Marriage: The Rideout Case; Wallenberg: A Hero's Story-
1984; Someone I Touched (ABC); mini-
series: The Martian Chronicles-1979;
Space (CBS miniseries)-1985

BERGER, Robert and
BRODKIN, Herbert
  Business: Titus Productions
  211 East 51st Street
  New York, NY 10022
  Tel.: (212) 752-6460

credits:
m.o.w.'s include: Sakarov (HBO)-1985;
Doubletake (4 hr. m.o.w.)(CBS)-1987

BERNSTEIN, Jay
  Bus.: Jay Bernstein Productions
  Columbia Plaza
  Burbank, CA 91505
  Tel.: (818) 954-3791

credits:
as executiver producer: Wild, Wild
West Revisited-1980; More Wild, Wild
West-1980; Micky Spillanes's Margin
For Murder-1981; Mike Hammer
Murder Me, Murder You-1983; series:
Bring 'Em Back Alive (CBS)-1982-83;
Mike Hammer-1984-85; The New Mike
Hammer (CBS)-1986-87; Houston
Knights (execuitve Producer)-1987

BERNSTEIN, Jonathan
  Bus.: 8970 Wonderland Park
  Los Angeles, CA 90046
  Tel.: (213) 650-8558

credits:
m.o.w.'s: Raisng Daisy Rothchild
(CBS); Running Out (CBS)-1983; Max
and Sam (CBS); On Fire (ABC); Can
You Fell Me Dancing? (NBC); Date
Night; *also, 4 features*

BLATT, Daniel
  Business: Blatt/Singer Productions
  Lorimar-Telepictures
  10202 W. Washington Blvd.
  Culver City, CA 90230

credits:
(co-productions with Robert
Singer)The Children Nobody Wanted-
1981; Sadat-1983; V -The Final Battle
(NBC)-1984; Sacred Vows(ABC)-1987

**BLOODWORTH-THOMASON,
Linda**
  Bus.: Mozark Productions
  c/o Columbia Pictures TV
  Columbia Plaza
  Burbank, CA 91505
  Tel.: (818) 954-4000

credits:
Designing Women (also creator & co-
executive producer with Harry
Thomason)(CBS)-1986-87

BOCHCO, Steven
  Office: 20th Century Fox
  Tel. (213) 277-2211

credits:
Hill Street Blues-1981-1986; L.A. Law
(Exec. Prod.)-1986-87.

BOROWITZ, Andy
  c/o UBU Productions
  5555 Melrose Avenue
  Los Angeles, CA 90038

credits:
series: as exec. producer: Easy Street-
1986-87; Day to Day (NBC)-1987

BOYETT, Bob
Miller/Boyett prodsuctions
c/o Lorimar-Telepictures
10202 W. Washington Blvd.
Culver City, CA 90230
Tel.: (213) 558-5000

credits:
as executive producer: Laverne &
Shirley; Happy Days; Bossom Buddies;
Mork & Mindy; Valerie (NBC)-1986-87

BRICE, John and Sandra
Bus.: Brice Productions
1643 Warnall Ave.
Los Angeles, CA 90024
Tel.: (213) 557-0366

credits:
LBJ: The Early Years (CBS m.o.w.)-
1987; LBJ: The White House Years
(CBS m.o.w.)-1987

BRILLSTEIN, Bernie
Bus.: Lorimar-Telepictures
10202 W. Washington Blvd.
Culver City, CA 90230
Tel.: (213) 202-2345
messages: (213) 275-6135

credits:
Burns & Schreiber; Ben Vereen Show;
Open All Night; Buffalo Bill (NBC);
Sitcom (HBO); Alf (exec. prod.)(NBC)-
1986-87; The Days and Nights of Molly
Dodd (NBC)-1987; It's Gary
Shandling's Show (Showtime)-1987;
Slap Maxwell (ABC)-1987; Puppetman
(CBS)-1987
*currently Chairman & CEO of Lorimar
Film Entertainment*

CANNELL, Stephen J.
Bus. The Cannell Studios
7083 Holywood Blvd.
Hollywood, CA 90028
Tel.: (213) 465-5800

credits:
Baa, Baa Black Sheep; The Rockford
Files; The A-Team-1983-86; Hunter-
1987

CARD, Lamar
Bus.: Card/Comtois
201 N. Robertson Drive #D
Beverly Hills, CA 90211
Tel.: (213) 273-1287

credits:
The Blood of Others (HBO min-series)
(exec.producer)-1986; producer on 4
features.

CARON, Glen Gordon
Bus.: Picturemaker Productions
20th Century Fox
10201 W. Pico Blvd.
Los Angeles, CA 90035
Tel.: (213) 203-1043

credits:
Murder She Wrote (CBS)-1984;
Moonlighting (ABC)-1985-87

CARSEY, Marcy
Bus.: Carsey-Werner Company
c/o NBC Studios
1268 14th Street
Brooklyn, New York 11230

credits:
The Cosby Show (exec. Prod. with
Tom Werner)(NBC)-1984-87

CHERONES, Tom
  Agent: Leading Artists
  Tel.: (213) 858-1999

credits:
series: The Two of Us (also writer)-
1981; Suzanne Pleshette Show; Berrin-
gers; Growing Pains; My Sister Sam
(CBS)-1987

CHRISTIANSEN, Robert W.
  Bus.: Chris-Rose Productions
  c/o Group W Productions
  3801 Barham Blvd., Suite 200
  Los Angeles, CA 90069
  Tel.: (213) 850-3879

credits:
(co-productions with Rick Rosenberg)
m.o.w.'s: Suddenly Single; Truman
Capote's The Glass House; Gargoyles;
The Man Who Could Talk to Kids; The
Autobiography of Miss Jane Pittman-
1974; Born Innocent; Queen of the
Stardust Ballroom; A Death In Canaan;
Strangers: The Story of a Mother and
Daughter; Robert Kennedy and His
Times (mini-series); Kid's Don't Tell;
As Summers Die (HBO)-1987

CLARK, Dick
  Bus.: dick clark productions
  3003 W. Olive Avenue
  Burbank, CA 91510
  Tel.: (818) 841-3003

credits include:
series: American Bandstand (ABC)-
1957-1987; Puttin' on the Hits; TV's
Bloopers & Practical Jokes; Captain &
Tennille; Dick Clark's Live Wednes-
day; Dick Clark Presents the Rock &
Roll Years; specials: New Year's
Rockin Eve; American Music Awards;
Superstars and Their Moms-1987;
Golden Globe Awards; Live Aid;
Academy of Country Music Awards;
m.o.w.'s: The Birth of the Beatles;
Murder In Texas; The Woman Who
Willed a Miracle; The Demon Murder
Case; Copacabana. *Chairman & c.e.o.
of dick clark productions, Inc.*

CONRAD, Robert
  Business: A Shane Co.
  21355 Pacific Coast Highway
  Malibu, CA 90265
  Tel: (213) 456-5655

credits:
m.o.w.'s: Will (NBC); Coach of the
Year (NBC); Hard Knox; High Mountain Rangers (CBS)-1987

CORDAY, Barbara
  Bus.: Columbia Pictures Television
  Columbia Plaza East #139
  Burbank, CA 91505
  Tel.: (818) 954-2637

*Barbara Corday is president of
Columbia Pictures / Embassy Television*

COSSETTE, Pierre
  Bus.: Pierre Cossette Productions
  8899 Beverly Blvd. # 900
  Los Angeles, CA 90048
  Tel.: (213) 278-3366

credits include:
numerous variety specials (Grammy
Awards); m.o.w.'s: Too Young A
Hero-1987

CRAMER, Douglas
Bus.: The Douglas Cramer Co.
Warner Hollywood Studios
1041 N. Formosa Blvd.
Los Angeles, CA 90046
Tel.: (213) 850-2661

credits:
As executive producer: The Love Boat;
Dynasty; Matt Houston; Hotel; Glitter;
MacGruder & Loud; Hollywood Wives
(mini-series)-1985; Hollywood Beat;
The Colbys-1986-87; Cracked Up
(m.o.w.)-1986

De CORDOVA, Fred
Bus.: The Tonight Show
NBC
3000 W.Alameda Ave.
Burbank, CA 91523
Tel.: (818) 840-4444

credits-series:
As director/producer: Donna Reed
Show; Bob Cummings Program;
Farmer's Daughter; Mr. Adams and
Eve; Burns and Allen; December Bride;
Jack Benny Program; as producer: The
Tonight Show-1971-1987.

De GUERE, Philip
Bus.Mgr.: Zane Lubin
Tel. (818) 905-9500

credits:
series: Simon and Simon; The Twilight
Zone (CBS)-1985-87

DEELEY, Michael
Bus.: Consolidated Productions
9000 Sunset Blvd., Suite 512
Los Angeles, CA 90069
Tel.: (213) 275-5719

credits:
m.o.w.: A Gathering of Old Men
(CBS)-1987; *features include The
Deerhunter and Blade Runner*

de PASSE, Suzanne
Bus.: Motown Productions
6255 Sunset Blvd.
Los Angeles, CA 90028
Tel.: (213) 461-9954

credits:
As executive producer: Motown 25;
Yesterday, Today, Forever; Motown
Returns to the Apollo; Nightlife; Fit for
Life; Motown on Showtime

Di BONA, Vicent J.
Bus.: Vin Di Bona Productions
4151 Prospect Avenue
Los Angeles, CA 90027
Agent: Sy Fischer Co.
Tel.: (213) 969-2900

credits:
Entertainment Tonight; On Stage
America; MacGyver; Animal Crack-
ups-1987

DIRECTOR, Roger
Office: 20th Century Fox
Tel.: (213) 277-2211

credits:
Moonlighting (ABC)-1987

DOTY, Dennis E.
Bus.: The Rule/Starger Co.
100 Universal City Plaza
Universal City, CA 91608
Tel.: (818) 777-1000

credits:
m.o.w.: Escape From Sobibor-1987

DUNNE, Cindy
Office: Cindy Dunne Prods.
2020 Avenue of the Stars
Suite 350
Los Angeles, CA 90067
Tel.: (213) 577-0204

*Former executive at Warner Bros. TV,
now developing features and longforms.*

ECKSTEIN, George
Bus: Schaefer/Karpf/Eckstein Prods.
3500 W. Olive Blvd.
Toluca Lake, CA 91505
(818) 953-7770

credits:
m.o.w.'s: Duel-1971; Banacek-1972;
Emelia Earhart-1974; 79 Park Avenue-
1978; Masada-1981; The Letter
(exec.prod.)-1981; Six Against the Rock
(NBC)-1987

EDWARDS, Ralph
Bus.: Ralph Edwards Productions
1717 N. Highland Ave, # 1018
Hollywood, CA 90028
Tel.: (213) 462-2212

credits include:
Truth or Consequences, This is Your
Life, Name That Tune, The People's
Court; This Is Your Life (special
edition)-1987

FEURY, Joe
Bus. : Joe Feury Productions
1776 Broadway
New York, NY 100
Tel: (212) 247-7965

credits:
Wanted: The Perfect Guy (ABC
Afternoon Special); What Sex Am I-
1985; Down and Out in America
(HBO) (Academy Award)-1986;
Nobody's Child-1986

FILERMAN, Michael
Office: Lorimar-Telepictures
3970 Overland Avenue
Culver City, CA 90230

credits:
Knots Landing (co-prod.)(CBS)-1987;
m.o.w.: Christmas Eve-1986

FINNEGAN, Bill
Bus.: The Finnegan-Pinchuk Co.
4225 Coldwater Canyon
Studio City, CA 91604
Tel.: (818) 985-0430

credits include:
series: The Days and Nights of Molly
Dodd (NBC)-1987; m.o.w.'s: Between
Two Brothers-1981; World War III-
1981; News at Eleven-1985; Golden
Harvest-1986; The Alamo (3 hrs.)-1986;
*features include Support Your Local
Gunfighter and North Shore*

FINNEGAN, Pat
  Bus.: The Finnegan-Pinchuk Co.
  Tel.: (818) 985-0430

credits include:
m.o.w.'s: This Child Is Mine; Baby Girl
Scott-1987

FRIES, Charles W.
  Bus.: Fries Entertainment
  6922 Hollywood Blvd.
  Los Angeles, CA 90028
  Tel.: (213) 466-2266
  Bus. contact: Tom Johnson
  Tel.: (213) 466-2266

credits:
m.o.w.'s: Toughlove; The Right of the
People; Intimate Strangers; Bitter
Harvest; A Rumor of War; Cocaine'
One Man's Addiction; Dempsey; A
Cry for Love; Blood Vows: The Story
of a Mafia Wife; The Alamo: 3 Days to
Glory; Fight For Life; Bridge to Silence;
Driving School; Intimate Betrayal; Two
Women; Drop Out Mother; LBJ: The
White House Years; The Crucible (CBS
mini-series); The Rose Kennedy Story
(CBS mini-series)
President of Fries Entertainment

GEIGER, George
  Bus. Michael Mann Productions
  100 Universal City Plaza
  Universal City, CA 91608

credits:
series: Simon & Simon; Scarecrow and
Mrs. King (exec. Producer); Miami
Vice (co-executive producer with
Michael Mann)-1987-88

GERBER, David
  Bus.: MGM/UA Television
  10000 W. Washington Blvd.
  Culver City, CA 90232
  Tel.: (213) 280-6000

credits include:
The Night the City Screamed; Beaulah
Land; Elvis and the Beauty Queen;
Terror Among Us; The Last Days of
Pompeii (mini-series); George Wash-
ington: The Forging of a Nation (mini-
series)(CBS)-1986
President of MGM/UATelevision

GOLDBERG, Gary David
  Bus.: UBU Productions
  Paramount Pictures
  5555 Melrose Avenue
  Los Angeles, CA 90038
  Tel. (213) 468-5000

credits:
Tony Randall Show (co-prod)-1978;
Lou Grant (Emmy)-1979; The Last
Resort; Family Ties-1981-1987; Day to
Day (NBC)-1987

GOLDBERG, Leonard
  Bus.: 20th Century Fox
  10201 W. Pico Blvd.
  Los Angeles, CA 90035
  Tel; (213) 277-2211

credits:
series: The Rookies-1972-76; Starsky &
Hutch-1975-79; Charlies Angeles-1976-
81; Family-1976-80; Fantasy Island-
1978-84; Hart to Hart-1979-84; T.J.
Hooker-1982-85; Paper Dolls-1984; The
Cavanaughs-1987; M.O.W.'s include:

GOLDBERG, continued

Brian's Song-1971; Letters From Three Lovers-1973; The Legend of Valentino-1975; The Boy In The Plastic Bubble-1976; This House Possessed-1981 Deadly Lessons-1982; Something About Amelia-1984; Alex; The Life of a Child-1987; *also produced 6 features Leonard Goldberg is President & Chief Operating Officer of 20th Century Fox*

GOLDWYN, Samuel Jr.
  Bus.: The Samuel Goldwyn Co.
  10203 Santa Monica Blvd.
  Los Angeles, CA 90067
  Tel.: (213) 552-2255

credits:
The Academy Awards-1987; April Morning (exec. producer)(CBS)-1987

GRAZER, Brian
  Bus.: Imagine Films Entertainment
  1925 Century Park East
  23rd Floor
  Los Angeles, CA 90067
  Tel.: (213) 277-1665

credits:
Ohara (ABC) (exec. Prod.)-1987; *features include Splash & Vibes*

GREENE, Vanessa
  Bus.: Vanessa Greene Productions
  c/o The Landsburg Company
  11811 W. Olympic Blvd.
  Los Angeles, CA 90064
  Tel.: (213) 478-7878

credits:
m.o.w.'s: Rape and Marriage: The Rideout Case-1980; Wait til Your Mother Gets Home-1982; Hobson's Choice-1983; Under the Influence(CBS)-1987

GROSSO, Sonny
  Bus.: Grosso-Jacobson Prods.
  767 Third Avenue, Fl. 15
  New York, NY 10017
  Tel.: (212)644-6909

credits:
m.o.w.'s include: Man of Honor Trackdown; Baker's Dozen; series: Night Heat; Hot Shots; The Gunfighters-1987

HALEY, Jack Jr.
  Bus.: Jack Haley, Jr. Prods.
  8255 Beverly Blvd.
  Los Angeles, CA 90048
  Tel.: (213) 655-1106

credits:
Hollywood, the Golden Years (with David Wolper); Believe It or Not (ABC)

HALMI, Robert
  Bus.: Robert Halmi
  Productions
  New York, NY

credits:
m.o.w.'s & miniseries: Pack of Lies-1987; Ford-The Man ans the Machine-1987; Mayflower Madam (CBS)-1987; April Morning (CBS)-1987; Grand Larceny

HAMILTON, Joe
Bus.: Joe Hamilton Productions
c/o Mama's Family
5746 Sunset Blvd.
Hollywood, CA 90028
Tel.: (213) 856-1717

credits:
Mama's Family-1982-1987

HARGROVE, Dean
office: Lorimar-Telepictures
10202 W. Washington Blvd.
Culver City, CA 90230
Tel.: (213) 558-6387

credits:
Columbo; McCloud; Name of the
Game; Madigan; Matlock (exec. prod)-
1986-88; m.o.w.'s: 4 Perry Mason
movies

HARRIS, Susan
Bus.: Witt/Thomas/Harris Prods.
1438 N. Gower Street.
Los Angeles, CA 90038
Tel.: (213) 464-1333

credits:
The Golden Girls (exec. producer)-
1985-87

HASBURGH, Patrick
Bus.: The Cannell Studios
7083 Hollywood Blvd.
Hollywood, CA 90028

credits:
as exec. producer: Hardcastle &
McCormick; 21 Jump Street (FBC)-1987

HERTZOG; Larry
Bus.: The Cannell Studios
7083 Hollywood Blvd.
Hollywood, CA 90028

credits:
as exec. producer: Starbuck; Hardcastle
& McCormick; Stingray

HILL, Leonard
Bus.: Leonard Hill Films
c/o Lorimar-Telepictures
10202 W. Washington Blvd.
Culver City, CA 90230
Tel.: (213) 558-6811

credits:
m.o.w.'s: Dream House-1981; Mae
West-1982; Having It All (ABC)-1983;
series: Rags To Riches (exec.
Prod.)(NBC)-1987

HILL, Tim
Bus.: Salkantay Productions
255 Maberry Road
Santa Monica, CA 90402
Tel.: (213) 454-1658

credits:
No Mean Tricks-1978; Pursuit of the
Marvelous-1981; Until Death-1986

HUGGINS, Roy
Bus.: Stephen J. Cannell Prods.
7083 Hollywood Blvd.
Hollywood, CA 90028
Tel.: (213) 465-5800

credits:
as creator & Exec. Producer: 77 Sunset
Strip; Maverick; The Fugitive; Alias

producers

HUGGINS, continued

Smith & Jones; The Rockford Files;
Blue Thunder; Hunter; The Last
Convertible (mini-series)

IRVING, Richard
Agent: Stephanie Rogers & Assoc.
Tel.: (818) 509-1010

credits include:
The Virginain; Istanbul Express;
Columbo; Seventh Avenue (mini-
series)-1977; Masada (prod. exec.)-
1979; The Last Days of Pompeii (mini-
series)-1983; Wallenberg: A Hero's
Story (NBC min-series)-1984

ISENBERG, Gerald
Bus.: Phoenix Entertainment
310 San Vicente Blvd.,Ste. 300
Los Angeles, CA 90048
Tel.: (213) 657-7502

credits include:
as co-executive producer: Thompson's
Last Run (CBS); Monte Carlo (CBS
mini-series)-1986

JACOBS, David
Office: Lorimar-Telepictures
3970 Overland Ave.
Culver City, CA 90230
Tel. (213) 558-5000

credits:
Knots Landing (co-prod.)-1987

KALLIS, Stanley

credits:
m.o.w.'s: Airwolf; Kane & Abel (CBS
mini-series)-1985

KATZMAN, Leonard
Bus.: Lorimar-Telepictures
3970 Overland Avenue
Culver City, CA 90230
Tel.: (213) 558-5000

credits:
Gunsmoke; Petrocelli; Dallas (executive producer) (CBS)-1984-1987

KEEGAN, Terry
Bus.: Fellows/Keegan Productions
11811 W. Olympic Blvd.
Los Angeles, CA 90024
Tel.: (213) 478—7878

credits:
m.o.w.'s include: One Shoe Makes It
Murder; The Girl, The Gold Watch,
and Everything; Top of the Hill; The
Gold Crew-1986

KELLER, Max
Bus.: Inter Planetary Pictures
14225 Ventura Blvd.
Sherman Oaks, CA 91423
Tel.: (818)981-4950

credits:
m.o.w.'s as executive producer:
Stranger in Our House-1978; Kent
State-1981; Gramblings White Tiger-
1982; A Summer to Remember-1985;
Betrayed by Innocence-1986; Dreams
of Gold-1986; Conspiracy: The Trial of
the Chicago 8-1987

KELLER, Micheline
Bus.: Inter Plantetary Pictures
Tel.: (818) 981-4950

credits:
m.o.w.'s: Stranger In Our House
(exec.prod.)-1978; Kent State
(exec.prod)-1981; Grambling's White
Tiger-1982; A Summer to Remember-
1985; Betrayed by Innocence-1986;
Dreams of Gold (supervising prod.)-
1986; Conspiracy: The Trial of the
Chicago 8-1987

KERNER, Jordan
Bus.: Avnet/Kerner Co.
505 N. Robertson Blvd.
Los Angeles, CA 90048
Tel.: (213) 271-7408

*Partnered with Jonathan Avnet for
television & Features*

KOSTROFF, Larry
c/o H. Roy Matlin & Associates
16027 Ventura Blvd.
Encino, CA 91436

credits:
The Penalty Phase (prod. mgr)-1986;
numerous feature credits

KOZOLL, Michael
Bus.: GTG Entertainment
9336 W. Washington Blvd.
Culver City, CA 90230
Tel.: (213) 836-5537

credits:
Hill Street Blues (created)

KRAGEN, Ken
Bus.: Kragen & Company
1112 N Sherbourne Dr.
Los Angeles., CA 90069
Tel.: (213) 854-4400

credits:
m.o.w.'s: as executive producer: Kenny
Roger's as the Gambler; Coward of the
County; The Gambler II; The Gambler
III-1987

KRAMER, Kenyon
office: Viacom Enterprises
10 Universal City Plaza
Universal City, CA 91608
Tel.:(818)505-7500

credits:
Tribute To Hermes Pan (also
writer)(CBS)-1986
*Currently Director of Program Devel-
opment and Productions*

KUKOFF, Bernie
(also, see Writers)
Office: Columbia Pictures TV
Columbia Plaza
Burbank, CA 91505
Tel.: (818) 954-6000

credits include:
series: T.J Hooker (pilot); Tucker's
Witch (CBS); Reggie (ABC); New Dick
Van Dyke Show (exec.prod.); Rags to
Riches (exec.prod.)(NBC)-1987; Lt.
Shuster's Wife (NBC m.o.w.)

producers

LANDSBURG, Alan
Bus.: The Landsburg Co.
11811 W. Olympic Blvd.
Los Angeles, CA 90064
Tel.: (213) 478-7878

credits:
Biography; Nation Geographic Specials (exec. producer)-1965-1970; The Undersea World of Jacques Costeau (exec. prod.); In Search Of....; That's Incredible; Adam (m.o.w.); Fear on Trial (m.o.w.); Parent Trap II-1986; Adam: His Song Continues (NBC); The George McKenna Story (CBS)-1986; Long Gone (HBO)-1987

LANSING, Sherry
Bus.: Jaffe-Lansing Productions
5555 Melrose Avenue
Los Angeles, CA 90048
Tel.: (213) 468-4515

credits:
m.o.w.: exec.produer with Stanley Jaffe: When the Time Comes-1987, *features include Racing With the Moon*

LARSON, Glen
Bus.: Glen Larson Productions
10201 W. Pico Blvd.
Los Angeles, CA 90035
Tel.: (213) 203-1076

credits:
series: Quincy; McCloud; Magnum P.I. (created); The Fall Guy; Knight Rider; The Highway Man (NBC)(exec.prod.)-1987

LAW, Lindsey
Business: American Playhouse
Public Television Playhouse
1776 Broadway
New York, NY 10019

credits include:
Forget-Me-Not-Lane; Beyond the Horizon; The Time of Your Life; Ah! Wilderness; The Good Doctor; You Can't It With You; The Girls In Their Summer Dress; For Colored Girls...; Working; Blue Window; Concealed Enemies (exec. prod.)(Emmy Award)-1984; Rachel River; The Silence At Bethany; plus executive produced over 80 programs for American Playhouse.

LEAR, Norman
Bus.: Act III Communications
1800 Century Park East
Suite 200
Los Angeles, CA 90067
Tel.:(213) 553-3636

credits:
series: All In the Family (4 Emmy awards); Maude; The Jeffersons; Sanford & Son; Mary Hartman; One Day At A Time; m.o.w.: Heartsounds (exec. prod.)-1985; *numerous feature films*

LEIDER, Jerry
Bus.: ITC Enyertainment
12711 Ventura Blvd.
Studio City, CA91604
Tel.: (818)760-2110

credits:
m.o.w.'s: Willa (exec. prod.); Hostage Tower (exec.prod.); The Scarlet & The

NEW WORLD TELEVISION GROUP

LEIDER, continued

Black; Secrets of a Married Man; The
Haunting Passion; Letting Go; A Time
to Live; A Time to Live; The Girl Who
Spelled Freedom; Unnatural Causes;
Poor Little Rich Girl (mini-series)
President ond CEO of ITC Entertainment

LEESON, Michael

(Also, see Writers)
credits:
I Married Dora (exec. prod.)-1987

LEVY, Franklin

Bus.: Catalina Production
Group, Ltd.
4421 Riverside Drive, Ste. 100
Burbank, CA 91505
Tel.: (818) 841-9797

credits:
The Last Hurrah (NBC); Enola Gay
(exec. prod.)(NBC)-1980; The Day the
Bubble Burst (exec. prod.)-1981; co-
productions with Gregory Harrison:
For Ladies Only (NBC)-1982;
Thursday's Child (exec.prod.)(CBS)-
1982; Legs (ABC)-1983; The Fighter
(CBS)-1983; Journey's End (Showtime)-
1983; Samson & Delilah (ABC)-1984;
Seduced (CBS)-1985; Pleasures (ABC)-
1986; Ocean's of Fire-1986; The Christ-
mas Star; Spot Mark's the X (Disney
Channel)-1987; Hot Paint (CBS)-1987

LOCKE, Peter

Bus.: Atlantic Kushner-Locke, Inc.
10880 Wilshire Blvd., 24th fl.
Los Angeles, CA 90024
Tel.: (213) 470-0400

credits:
series: The Stockard Channing Show-
1979-80; Automan (ABC)-1983;
m.o.w.'s: Silent Victory (co-prod. with
David Debin)-1979; Love At First Sight
(CBS)-1980; Two For Two-1980; A Gun
in the House (with Debin)-1981; The
Star Maker (NBC)-1981; Contraption
(Disney Channel)-1983; First & Ten
(HBO)-1985-87

MANDABACH, Caryn

Bus.: Carsy-Werner
Productions
5800 Sunset Blvd.
Los Angeles, CA 90028
Tel.: (213) 460-5500

credits:
Operation Petticoat; The Cosby Show-
1983-86
President of Carsey-Werner Productions

MANN, Michael

Bus.: Michael Mann Co.
c/o Universal Studios,
Bldg. 69
100 Universal City Plaza
Universal City, CA 91608
Tel.: (818) 777-1112

credits:
series: Miami Vice (exec. prod.)-1985-87; Crime Story (exec.prod.)(NBC)-1986-87

MANSON, David
Bus.: Sarabande Productions
9454 Wilshire Blvd., Ste. 309
Beverly Hills, CA 90212
Tel.: (213) 278-1604

credits:
The Spell (NBC)-1976; A Rumor of War (CBS mini-series)-1980; The Word (CBS)-1980; A Love Affair-The Eleanor and Lou Gehrig Story (NBC)-1981; Night Cries (ABC); Sessions (NBC)-1985; Best Kept Secrets (ABC); *also produced 2 features: Bring on the Night and Birdy*

MANULIS, Martin
Martin Manulis Productions Ltd.
P.O. Box 818
Beverly Hills, CA 90210
Tel. (213) 476-2709

credits include:
Playhouse 90, Requiem For A Heavyweight, The Miracle Worker, The Comedian; Dobie Gillis (series); Adventures in Paradise (series); James at 15 (m.o.w.); Chiefs (CBS mini-series)-1983; James Michener's Space (CBS mini-series)-1984
Currently Artistic Director for the Ahmanson Theater

MARGULIES, Stan
Bus.: The Stan Margulies Co.
c/o Telecom Entertainment
6500 Wilshire Blvd.
Los Angeles, CA 90048
Tel.: (213) 858-4525

credits:
Roots-1976; Roots: The Next Generations-1978; Moviola-1980; The Thorn Birds (mini-series)-1982; Sparkling Cyanide-1983; Embassy (ABC)-1985; A Bunny's Tale (ABC)-1986; Out on a Limb (mini-series)-1987

McCLAIN, Chuck
Bus.: ITC Produtions
12711 Ventura Blvd.
Studio City, CA 91604
Tel.: (818) 760-2110

credits:
Dream West-1985; North and South, Book I (executive producer)-1985; Nutcracker: Money, Madness, and Murder (exec. prod.)(mini-series)-1986

McMAHON, John
Bus.: John Mc Mahon Productions
c/o MGM/UA
10000 W. Washington Blvd.
Culver City, CA 90232
Tel.: (213) 280-6000

credits:
As executive producer: m.o.w.'s: Mercy of Murder; John & Yoko; Passions; Fire on the Mountain; If It's Tuesday, It Must Be Belgium-1987; My

producers

McMAHON, continued

Father, My Son-1987; Starmaker (mini-series); series: Cassie & Co.; Teachers Only; Partners In Crime

McNEELY, Jerry
  (Also, see Writers)
  Office: Lorimar-Telepictures
  Tracy Bldg.
  10202 W. Washington
  Culver City, CA 90230
  Tel.: (213) 558-5000

credits:
m.o.w.'s: Something for Joey; The Critical List; The Boy Who Drank Too Much; Fighting Back: The Story of Rocky Blier: Tomorrow's Child; Trauma Center; Sin of Innocence (co-exec. prod)-1984; series: Our House (NBC)-1986-1988

METCALFE, Burt
  (Also, see directors)
  Agent: Broder-Kurland-Webb
  Tel.: (213) 656-9262
  Office: CBS/MTM
  Tel.: (818) 760-6148

credits:
M*A*S*H (exec. producer)-1974-1981; AfterMASH-1982

MEYER, Irwin
  Bus.: Pound Ridge Prod'ns, Ltd.
  4000 Warner Blvd.
  Prods. 6, suite C
  Burbank, CA 91505
  Tel.: (818) 954-3371

credits:
as exec.producer with Stephen R. Friedman: In Love With an Older Woman (CBS); The Canterville Ghost; It Almost Wasn't Christmas-1987

MILCH, David

credits:
Hill Street Blues (exec. prod.)-1987

MILKIS, Edward
  Bus.: Ed Milkis Productions
  5555 Melrose Avenue
  Los Angeles, CA 90038
  Tel.: (213) 468-5901

credits:
Happy Days (exec.prod.)-1974-82; Bosom Buddies (exec. prod.); Laverne & Shirley (exec. prod.)

MILLER, Tom
  Bus.: Miller/Boyett Productions
  3970 Overland Avenue
  Culver City, CA 90230
  Tel.: (213) 558-5000

credits:
as executive producer: Happy DAys; Laverne & Shirley; Bossom Buddies; Valerie-1987

MONTY, Gloria
  Bus.: Gloria Monty Productions
  c/o 20th Century Fox
  10201 W. Pico Blvd.
  Los Angeles, CA 90035
  Tel.:(213) 203-1214

MONTY, continued

credits:
General Hospital (executive prod.)(2 Emmy awards)-1977-86; The Hamptons (exec.prod.)-1983-85; Confessions of a Married Man -1982; The Imposter-1984
Currently Executive Producer at 20th Century Fox in development for primetime TV.

MORSE, Terry
P.O. Box 3763
Beverly Hill, CA 90212
Tel.: (213)277—2747

credits:
m.o.w.'s: Freedom; Mae West; The Imposter; Peyton Place, The Next Generation; A Letter to Three Wives; A Masterpiece of Murder (NBC)-1986

MUMFORD, Thad
(also, see Writers)
Agent: Leading Artists
Tel.: (213) 858-1999

credits:
M*A*S*H (4 yrs.); The Duck Factory (NBC)-1984; Alf (exec. producer)(NBC)-1986-87

NEUFELD, Mace
Bus.: Mace Neufeld Productions
9454 Wilshire Blvd, 6th floor
Beverly Hills, CA 90212
Tel.: (213) 278-3034

credits:
Laugh Line (NBC); Captain & Tenille (exec.prod. (ABC); Cagney & Lacey (ABC m.o.w.); John Steinbeck's East of Eden (ABC miniseries); Angel on my Shoulder (ABC m.o.w.); The American Dream (ABC series); A Death In California (exec. prod.) (ABC miniseries); The Flying Karamazov Brothers (Showtime); Production company is in association with Cagney & Lacey series.

NEWLAND, John
Bus.: Newland-Raynor Prods.
8480 Beverly Blvd. #133
Los Angeles, CA 90048
Tel. (213) 655-2222

credits:
A Sensitive, Passionate Man; Overboard-1980; Angel City; The Five of Me; Timestalker (CBS)-1987

O'CONNOR, Dick
Bus.: ABC Circle Films
9911 West Pico Bl.
Los Angeles, CA 90035
Tel. (213) 557-7777

credits:
m.o.w.'s include: Rage of Angels; Mini-series: Amerika (ABC)-1987.

OHLMEYER, Don
Bus.: Ohlmeyer Communications
962 N. LaCienega Blvd.
Los Angeles, CA 90069
Tel.: (213) 659-8557

credits:
m.o.w's: Cry of Innocence; Under Siege; Special Bulletin; 39th Annual

OHLMEYER, continued

Primetime Emmy Awards-1987; produced the 1972 & 1976 Summer Olympics

OVITZ, Mark
 Bus.: Mark Ovitz Productions
 Walt Disney Studios
 500 S. Buena Vista St.
 Burbank, CA 91521
 Tel.:(818) 840-1000

credits:
m.o.w.s: I-Man; B.R.A.T. Patrol; First Flight; Double Agent; You Ruined My Life-1987

PALTROW, Bruce
 Bus.: MTM
 CBS/MTM Studios
 Tel.: (818) 760-5000

credits:
series: St. Elsewhere (executive producer)(NBC)-1982-1987

PAPAZIAN, Robert
Bus.: Robert Papazian Prods.
9911 West Pico Blvd., Ste.600
Los Angeles, CA 90067
Tel.: (213) 277-1160

credits: m.o.w's include: Grass Roots (NBC); Murder By Natural Causes (CBS); Topper (ABC); Stand Bt Your Man (CBS); Intimate Agony (ABC); My Life, Your Life (NBC); Guilty Conscience (CBS); The Ray "Boom Boom" Mancini Story (CBS); Crisis At Central High (CBS); The Day After (ABC)

(Emmy nom.)-1983; Love Among Thieves (ABC); Kate's Secret (NBC)-1986; The Betty Ford Story (ABC)-1987; The United States of America vs. Salim Ajami (CBS)-1987. *Robert Papazian has received seven Emmy awards.*

PARKER, Jim
(also, see Writers)
Agent: Stephanie Rogers & Assoc.
3855 Lankershim Blvd. # 218
North Hollywood, CA 91604
Tel.: (818) 509-1010

credits: Love, American Style (4yrs.); Love Sidney (Emmy nom.); Star of the Family

PARRIOTT, James
 Bus.: New World Televison
 1440 S. Sepulveda
 Los Angeles, CA 90025
 Tel: (213) 444-8100

credits:
The Incredible Hulk, The Legend of the Golden Gun; The Dobermans; From Here to Eternity (mini-series); Voyagers; Misfits of Science-1986

PETRIE, Dorothea G.

credits:
Orphan Train-1979; Angel Dusted-1981; Lincense to Kill-1984; Picking Up The Pieces-1985; Love Is Never Silent-1985; Foxfire (CBS m.o.w.)-1987

PHILLIPS, Clyde
Bus.: Columbia Pictures Television
4000 Warner Blvd.
Producers 6
Burbank, CA 91505
Tel.:(818)-954-6000

credits:
series; Trapper John M.D.; Midas
Valley-1985; Houston Knights
(CBS)(supervising producer)-1987;
m.o.w.'s: Queen of the Stardust
Ballroom (assoc. prod.); If Things Were
Different (CBS); Bud & Lou (NBC);
Charles & Diana: A Royal Love Story
(ABC); Not In Front of the Children
(CBS) (supervising producer); Ob-
sessed With a Married Woman (ABC)

POMPIAN, Paul
Bus.: Pompian-Atamian Prods.
9035 Venice Blvd., 2nd Floor
Culver City, CA 90035
Tel.: (213) 202-6206

credits:
m.o.w.'s: Death of a Centerfold: The
Dorthy Stratton Story (NBC)-1981;
Hear No Evil(CBS)-1982; Through
Naked Eyes (ABC)-1983; I Want to
Live (ABC)-1983; Deadly Messages
(ABC)-1984; Silent Witness (NBC)-
1985;The Hearst & Davies Affair -1984;
Shattered Spirits (ABC) (mini-series)-
1986; Stepford Children (NBC)-1986;
True Colors-1987; series: Once A Hero
(ABC)-1987-88

RANKIN, Arthur
Bus.: Rankin & Bass
Productions

1 East 53rd Street
New York, NY 10022
Tel.: (212) 759-7721

credtis:
m.o.w.'s: (co-productions with Jules
Bass): The Sins of Dorian Gray; The
Flight of the Dragons; The Wind In the
Willows
*Rankin & Bass Productions are associ-
ated with Lorimar-Telepictures*

REES, Marian
Bus.: Marian Rees Associates
4125 Radford Avenue
Studio City, CA 91604
Tel.: (818) 508-5599

credits:
The Marva Collins Story-1981; Miss All
American Beauty-1982; Between
Friends-1983; License To Kill-1984;
Love Is Never Silent-1985;Resting
Place-1986; Christmas Snow-1986;
Foxfire (exec. prod.)(CBS)-1987; The
Room Upstairs-1987; Love Is Never
Silent (Emmy)-1986

RICH, John
Bus.: John Rich Enterprises
c/o Paramount Pictures
5555 Melrose Avenue
Los Angeles, CA 90038

credits:
All in the Family-1973; Macguyver-
1985-87

producers

ROSEMONT, David
Bus.: Rosemont
Productions,LTD
1990 Westwood Blvd., Suite 200
Los Angeles, CA 90025
Tel.: (213) 474-4700

credits:
m.o.w.'s: The Master of the Game, part
1; The Corsican Brothers-1985; The
Christmas Gift-1986

ROSEMONT, Norman
Bus.: Rosemont Productions
1990 Westwood Blvd. #200
Los Angeles, CA 90025
Tel.: (213) 474-4700

credits include:
m.o.w.s: The Man Without a Country-
1973; The Count of Monte Cristo-1975;
The 28th Annual Emmy Awards-1977;
Captains Courageous; All Quiet on the
Western Front-1979; Little Lord
Fauntleroy-1980; The Hunchback of
Notre Dame-1981; Master of the Game-
1983; Camille-1985; The Secret Garden-
1987

ROSENBERG, Rick
Bus.: Chris/Rose Productions
3801 Barham Blvd.
Los Angeles, CA 90068
Tel.: (213) 850-3879

credits:
co-productions with Bob Christiansen:
m.o.w.'s: Suddenly Single; The Glass
House; A Brand New Life; The Man
The Autobiography of Miss Jane
Pittman; I Love You, Goodbye; Born
Innocent; Queen of the Stardust
Ballroom; A Death In Canaan; Strang-
ers; Robert Kennedy and His Times;
Kid's Don't Tell; As Summers Die
(HBO)

ROSENZWEIG, Barney
Bus.: Rosenzweig Productions
2630 Lacy Street
Los Angeles, CA 90031
Tel.: (213) 222-8160

credits:
series: Cagney & Lacey (exec. producer)-1981-87; m.o.w.'s: Angel on my
Shoulder-1980; American Dream-1981;
East of Eden-1981; This Girl for Hire-
1983

RUDOLPH, Louis
Bus.: Lou Rudolph Productions
c/o Fries Entertainment
6922 Hollywood Blvd., 11 fl.
Los Angeles, CA 90028
Tel.:(213) 466-2266

credits:
M.O.W.s: A Case of Rape; The Dr. Sam
Shephard Murder Case; The Come-
back Kid; Attica (emmy award);
Jacqueline Bouvier Kennedy; Blood
Vows: Story of a Mafia Wife; LBJ: The
Early Years (exec. prod.)-1987; Mini-
series: Ike-1979; Deceptions; Jenny's
War; LBJ: The White House Years-1988

RULE, Elton
Bus.: The Rule/Starger Co.
100 Universal Ciyt Plaza
Universal City, CA 91608

*Mr. Rule was President and Chief
Operating Officer of the American
Broadcasting Companies from 1972-
1983.*

SAMUELS, Ron
Bus.: Ron Samuels Productions
1040 N. Las Palmas
Los Angeles, CA 90038
Tel: (213) 273-8964

credits:
m.o.w.'s include: The Last Song; The
Two World's of Jennie Logan; Scruples
(mini-series); The Incredible Journey of
Dr. Meg Laurel; Reachout; Two Kinds
of Lonliness; A Different Affair (CBS)-
1987

SCHERICK, Edgar
Bus.: Edgar J. Scherick Associates
10900 Wilshire Blvd., Suite 2300
Los Angeles, CA 90024
Tel.: (213) 473-7730

credits include:
m.o.w.'s: The Man Who Wanted to
Live Forever-1970; The Silence-1975;
Circle of Children-1977; Raid on
Entebbe (3hrs.);Panic in Echo Park-
1977; Zuma Beach-1978; An American
Christmas Carol-1979; The Seduction
of Miss Leona-1980; Revenge of the
Stepford Wive-1980; Hitler's S.S.-1985;
The High Price of Passion-1986; The
Stepford Children-1987; Unholy

Matrimony-1987; mini-series: Little
Gloria...Happy at Last-1983;
Evergreen-1985; On Wings of Eagles-
1986; Hands of a Stranger-1987; Home
Fires (Showtime)-1987; documentary:
He Makes Me Feel Like Dancin'
(Emmy & Academy award)-1983

SCHILLER, Lawrence
Bus.: Lawrence Schiller Prods.
P.O. Box 5784
Sherman Oaks, CA 91413
Tel.: (818) 906-0926

credits:
mini-series: Peter the Great-1986

SCHLATTER, George
Bus.: George Schlatter Prods.
321 Beverly Blvd.
Los Angeles, CA 90048
Tel.: (213) 655-1400

credits:
Real People; The American Comedy
Awards-1987

SEEGER, Susan
(also, see Writers)
Office: Paramount
5555 Melrose Avenue
Los Angeles, CA 90038
Tel.: (213) 468-5605

credits-series:
Duet (FBC) (executive prod. with Ruth
Bennett)-1987

SERTNER, Robert M.
Bus.: von Zerneck/Samuels
 Productions
12001 Ventura Place # 400

SERTNER, continued

Studio City, CA 91604
Tel.: (818) 766-2610

credits :
Answers (CBS); m.o.w.'s: Baby Sitter
(ABC); Night Partners (CBS); Police
Woman Centerfold (NBC); Police
Woman Centerfold (NBC); Obsessive
Love (CBS); Invitation to Hell (ABC);
Summer Fantasy (NBC); I Married A
Centerfold (NBC); Challenge of a
Lifetime (ABC); Hinal Jeopardy (NBC);
Hostage Flight (NBC); Combat High
(NBC); Queenie (ABC mini-series); Tall
Men (ABC); Celebration Family (ABC);
Trouble in the City of Angels (NBC);
To Heal a Nation (NBC)

SHANKS, Ann
Bus. Mgr. Rudnick, Lazarow
9107 Wilshire Blvd.
Beverly Hills, CA 90210
Tel.: (213) 273-8900

credits:
A Day In the Country (PBS); He's
Fired, She's Hired (CBS m.o.w.); Drop
Out Father (CBS m.o.w.)

SHANKS, Bob

credits include:
American Dream Machine; numerous
Emmy's

SHAPRIO, Esther
Office: Aaron Spelling Prods.
1041 N. Formosa Avenue
Los Angeles, CA 90046
Tel.: (213) 850-2770

credits:
m.o.w.'s: Sara T.: Portrait of a Teenage
Alcoholic; Minstral Man; Intimate
Strangers; series: Dynasty (co-exec.
producer with Richard Shapiro); The
Colby's (co-exec.producer)
*currently Senior Vice Pres. of Creative
Affairs for Aaron Spelling Productions*

SHAPIRO, Richard
Bus. Richard Shapiro Productions
1041 N. Formosa Avenue
Los Angeles, CA 90046
Tel.: (213) 850-2500

credits:
series: as co-executive producer:
Dynasty (ABC)-1983-87; The Colby's
(ABC)-1985-87

SILVERMAN, Fred
Bus.:Fred Silverman Co.
12400 Wilshire Blvd.
Los Angeles, CA 90025
Tel.: (213)826-6050

credits:
series: (as co-executive producer): We
Got It Made-1985-87; Matlock NBC)-
1985-87; Jake and the Fatman (CBS)-
1987-88; Braddock (NBC); m.o.w's:
Perry Mason Movies (four)(NBC)-1987;
A Father Dowling Mystery (NBC)-
1987; Pete Striker (HBO movie series)-
1987-88
*Fred Silverman has been a former chief
executive at NBC, ABC, and Vice Pres.
at CBS. He is currently President of
the Fred Silverman Company*

SINGER, Maurice
Bus.: Fries Entertainment
6922 Hollywood Blvd.
Los Angeles, CA 90028
Tel.: (213) 466-2266

credits:
The Last Innocent Man (HBO)-1986

SINGLETON, Ralph S.
Bus.: R.S. Singleton Productions
9903 Santa Monica Blvd.
Beverly Hills, CA 90212
Tel.: (213) 471-8066

credits:
Cagney & Lacey (also directed)-1986-87; UPM on numerous features

SMITH, Bruce
Tel.: (213) 459-6473

credits:
Indian Summer (A&E)-1985; Undercover-1987

SPELLING, Aaron
Bus.: Aaron Spelling Productions
Warner Hollywood Studios
1041 N. Formosa Avenue
Los Angeles, CA 90046
Tel.: (213) 850-2413

credits:
series include: The Rookies; Mod Squad; Starsky & Hutch; The Love Boat; Charlie's Angeles; Hart to Hart; T.J. Hooker; executive producer on numerous movies for TV.

STARGER, Martin
Bus.: Rule Starger Co.
100 Universal City Plaza
Universal City, CA 91608
Tel.: (818) 777-2055

credits include:
As executive producer: m.o.w.'s: Escape From Sobibor-1987; also numerous features

STEVENS, Bob
Bus.: Starry Night Produtions
c/o Warner Bros. Television
4000 Warner Blvd.
Burbank, CA 91522
Tel.: (818) 954-6000

credits:
Night Court (NBC)-1986-1987

STEVENS, George Jr.
Office: The American Film Institute
Kennedy Center for the
Performing Arts
Washington, D.C. 20566

credits include:
AFI Life Achievement Awards-1973-1987; The Kennedy Center Honors-1978-87; *has also produced numerous documentaries including A Filmmaker's Journey*

STRANGIS, Sam
Bus.: Ten-Four Productions
5555 Melrose Avenue
Los Angeles, CA 90038
Tel.: (213) 468-5000

producers

STRANGIS, continued

credits include:

m.o.w.'s: Rainbow(NBC)-1978; Off Sides (NBC)-1980; Rivkin: Bounty Hunter (CBS)-1981; Not Just Another Affair (CBS)-1982; He's Not Your Son (CBS)-1984; Stark (CBS)-1985; Chase (CBS)-1985; Mirror Image (CBS)-1986; Ghost of a Chance-1987; series: Harper Valley-1981-82; Little Miss Perfect (CBS Schoolbreak Special)-1986.

STUART, Malcolm
Bus.: Stuart Phoenix Productions
Lorimar-Telepictures
3970 Overland Avenue
Culver City, CA 90230
Tel.: (213) 558-5000

credits:

m.o.w.'s include: The Children of An Lac; A Cry for Love; One Shoe Makes It Murder; The Return of Will Kane; Washington Mistress; Two of a Kind; Johnny Belinda; Two of A Kind; The Winter of Our Discontent (Co-prod. with Gary Adelson)-1985; Why, Me; Lace; A Death In California; Christopher Columbis; Blloe and Orchids: Dallas: The Early Years; The Deliberate Stranger (exec. prod.); Ghost of A Chance (exec.prod.)-1987

SWERLING, Jo Jr.
Bus.: Stephen J. Cannell Prods.
7053 Hollywood Blvd.
Los Angeles, CA 90028

credits:
Hunter-1987; The A-Team-1987

TAFFNER, D.L.
Bus.: D.L. Taffner, Ltd.
5455 Wilshire Blvd., Ste.1980
Los Angeles, CA 90036
Tel.: (213) 937-1144

credits:
Three's Company; Too Close For Comfort

TAHSE, Martin
Bus.: Martin Tahse Productions
323 Veteran Avenue
Los Angeles, CA 90024
Tel.: (213) 476-7435

credits include:
Sara's Summer of the Swans(ABC)-1974; Francesca, Baby (ABC)-1976; Very Good Friends (ABC)-1977; It's A Mile From Here to Glory (ABC)-1978; Which Mother is Mine (ABC)-1979; What are Friends For (ABC)-1979; A Matter of Time (ABC)-1980; She Drinks A Little (ABC)-1981; Daddy, I'm A Mama Now (ABC)-1981; Andrea's Story: AHitchhiking Tragedy (ABC)-1982; The Hoken Chicken Emergency (PBS)-1984; Ace Hits The Big Time (CBS)-1985; A Desperate Exit (also directed)(ABC)-1986; Salem's Children-1986

TARSES, Jay
(also, see Writers)
Pers. Mgr.: Bernie Brillstein
Tel.: (213) 275-6135

TARSES, continued

credits:
series: as exec. producer: Buffalo Bill
(NBC); The Days and Nights of Mollie
Dodd (also created) (NBC)-1987

TATOR, Joel
Bus.: KCBS Television
6121 Sunset Blvd.
Los Angeles, CA 90028
Tel.: (213) 460-3000

credits:
2 On The Town (numerous Emmy
Awards); Friday At Sunset (exec.
producer)-1987

THOMAS, Tony
Bus.: Witt/Thomas Productions
1438 N. Gower St,
Los Angeles, CA 90028
Tel.: (213) 464-1333

credits:
Series as executive producer: Soap
(ABC) 1977-81; The Golden Girls
(NBC)-1986-87; It's A Living-1986-87;
One Big Family-1986-87

THOMPSON, Larry A.
Bus.: The Larry Thompson
Organization
1440 S. Sepulveda Blvd.
Los Angeles, CA 90025
Tel.: (213) 478-6100

credits:
m.o.w.s (as exec. producer): Mike
Hammer-Murder Me, Murder You-
1984; The Other Lover (CBS)-1985;

Convicted (ABC)-198; Intimate Encounter (ABC)-1986

THOMPSON, Tom
Bus.: KCET Television
4401 Sunset Blvd.
Los Angeles, CA 90027
Tel.: (213) 666-6500

credits include:
Prison of the Streets (PBS)-1987; KCET
Journal (executive Producer); California Stories (senior executive producer);
has received 8 Emmy awards

TISCH, Steve
Bus.: The Steve Tisch Co.
515 N. Robertson Blvd.
Los Angeles, CA 90048
Tel.: (213) 278-7680

credits:
m.o.w.'s: co-productions with Jon
Avnet: No other Love-1979; Prime
Suspect-1982; Something So Right-
1983; The Burning Bed-1984; Call to
Glory-1984; Silence of the Heart-1984;
as sole producer: In Love And War
(NBC)-1987; *features include Risky
Business, Soul Man, & Hot to Trot*

TURMAN, Lawrence
Bus.: Turman-Foster Company
c/o The Culver Studios
9336 W. Washington Blvd.
Culver City, CA 90230
Tel.: (213)202-3417

credits:
co-produced with David Foster: The
Gift of Life-1982; Between Two Broth-

producers

TURMAN, continued

ers-1982; She Lives-1984; News at Eleven-1985; *has produced numerous features including Short Circuit and Running Scared* .

VALENTE, Renee
Office: 2029 Century Park East
Suite 2500
Los Angeles, CA 90067
Tel.: (213) 201-7207
Agent: Lou Pitt, ICM

credits:
m.o.w.'s: The Last Hurrah; Brian's Song; Q.B. VII; Caryl Chessman Story; Contract on Cherry Street-1976; Blind Ambition (8 hrs.)-1979; Swan Song-1980; Valley of the Doll's (5 hrs.)-1981; Father Knows Best-Reunion; Love Thy Neighbor; Shattered-If Your Kid's on Drugs; Sin of Innocence; Poker Alice; Hit n' Run; series: Hawk; Masquerade-1983

VANOFF, Nick
Bus.: Sunset-Gower Studios
1438 N. Gower Street
Los Angeles, CA 90028
Tel. (213) 467-1001

credits include:
The Hollywood Palace-1964-1970; The Julie Andrews Hour (Emmy Award), The Kennedy Center Honors (co-produced with George Stevens, Jr.) (Emmy Award); The Big Show (NBC); On Stage, America.

VON ZERNECK, Frank
von Zerneck/Samuels Productions
12001 Ventura Place # 400
Studio City, CA 91604
Tel.: (818) 766-2610

credits:
m.o.w's include: As producer or executive producer: 21 Hours At Munich; Portrait of an Escort; Miracle On Ice; Lois Gibbs and the Love Canal-1982; In the Custody of Strangers-1982; The First Time-1982; Baby Sister-1983; Policewoman Centerfold-1983; Obsessive Love; Invitation to Hell-1984; Summer Fantasy-1984; Romance on the Orient Express-1985; Hostage Flight-1985; Final Jeopardy-1985; Dress Gray (mini-series)-1985; The Tall Men-1987; Trouble in the City of Angels (ABC)-1987

WEINBERGER, Ed
Bus.: Carson Productions
c/o Paramount, Bldg. F
5555 Melrose Avenue
Los Angeles, CA 90038
Tel.: (213) 468-5000

credits:
as executive producer: Taxi (with Stan Daniels)-1977-83; Mr. Smith-1983; Mr. President (FBC)-1987; Amen (NBC)-1987

WEITZ, Barry
Bus.: Barry Weitz Films
c/o New World Television
1440 Sepulveda Blvd.
Los Angeles, CA 90025

VIACOM

PRODUCTIONS

producers

WEITZ, continued

Tel.: (213) 444-8489

credits:
m.o.w.'s: Desperate Voyage-1980;
Time Bomb-1982; Lady From Yesterday; Riviera (ABC)-1987

WINITSKY, Alex
Bus.: Lantana Productions
9720 Wilshire Blvd., Ste. 706
Beverly Hills, CA 90212
Tel.: (213) 274-2761

credits:
Ford-The Man and the Machine (4hr. mini-series)-1987, *numerous features*

WINKLER, Henry
Bus.: Winkler/Daniel Productions
c/o Paramount Pictures
5555 Melrose Avenue
Los Angeles, CA 90038
Tel.: (213) 468-5700

credits:
series: Ryan's Four; Mr. Sunshine (NBC)-1985-86; Macguyver (ABC)-1985-87; The Last Flight of Starflight 1(m.o.w.)-1983; All The Kids Do It (Afterschool special, also directed)-1986

WITT, Paul Junger
Bus.: Witt/Thomas Productions
1438 Gower Street
Los Angeles, CA 90028
Tel.: (213) 464-1333

credits:
Series as executive producer: Soap (ABC)-1977-81; It's A Living-1987, The Golden Girls (NBC)-1986-87

WOLPER, David L.
Bus.Daivd L. Wolper Productions
4000 Warner Blvd.
Burbank, CA 91522
Tel.: (818) 954-1707

credits include:
series: Hollywood and the Stars; Biography; specials: The Making of a President, 1960 and 1968 (4 Emmy Awards); The Rise and Fall of the Third Reich; A Thousand Days; National Geographic Specials; They've Killed President Lincoln-1971; Appointment With Destiny (mult. Emmy Awards); Visions of Eight; m.o.w.'s: The Morning After-1974; The Court-Martial of Lt. Calley; I Will Fight No More Forever; Victory at Entebbe!-1976; Murder is Easy-1982; The Betty Ford Story (exec. prod.)-1987, mini-series: Roots (ABC)-1977; Roots: The Next Generations-1978; Moviola (NBC)-1979; The Thorn Birds-1982; North and South-1985; North and South, Book II-1986; Napoleon and Josephine: A Love Story (ABC mini-series)-1987
Mr. Wolper was the executive producer of the 1984 Olympic Games and the Statue of Liberty Celebration in New York City in 1986. Has won an Academy Award and over 40 Emmy awards. Also, received the Jean Hersholt Humanitarian Award in 1985.

ZANUCK, Richard
 Bus.: The Zanuck/Brown Co.
 202 N. Canon Drive
 Beverly Hills, CA 90210
 Tel.: (213) 274-5929

credits:
Barrington (exec.producer with David
Brown)(CBS)-1987

ZINBERG, Michael
 (also see Directors)
 Bus.: American Flyer Films
 10201 W. Pico Blvd.
 Los Angeles, CA 90035
 Tel.: (213) 201-1441
 Agent: Broder-Kurland-Webb

credits:
series: The Yellow Rose; Fathers and
Sons; Heart of the City (exec. prod.)-

SELZNICK
HOME
VIDEO

NEW YORK   CULVER CITY

WRITERS

ABATEMARCO, Frank
  Agent: Leading Artists
  Tel.: (213) 858-1999

credits:
m.o.w.'s: Day of the Rope (CBS)-1985;
The Sexiest Girl in the World (ABC);
Will (NBC); Coach of the year (NBC);
series: Black Sheep Squadron; Eischied

ALLEN, Jay Presson
  Agent: Jeff Berg, ICM
  Tel.: (213) 550-4000

credits:
Family (created)-1977; Clinic (ABC)-
1987

BAILY, Anne Howard
  Agent: Paramuse Artists Assoc.
  Tel.: (212) 758-5055

credits:
Halfway Home; How to Survive a
Marriage (ABC); Swifty (NBC); In
Search Of Love (NBC); Will There
Really be a Morning-1983; General
Hospital (head writer)(ABC)

BANTA, Gloria
  Agent: Lenny Rosenberg
  Wm. Morris Agency
  Tel.: (213) 274-7451
  c/o Highgate Pictures
  New York

credits:
Mary Tyler Moore-1974-75; Rhoda-
1974-77; Angie (also producer)-1980;
It's A Living (also producer)-1980-81;
Cagney & Lacey-1982; Executive-V.P.
Comedy Development, Paramount TV

1982-84. *Currently in development
with LCA/Highgate Pictures*

BARRETT, James Lee
  Agent: Sylvia Hirsch
  Sy Fischer Company
  Agency
  3330 Cahuenga Blvd.
  Los Angeles, CA 90068
  Tel.: (213) 969-2900

credits:
series: Our House (NBC)-1986-87;
m.o.w.'s: The Defiant Ones (ABC);
April Morning; The Day Christ Died;
Stubby Pringle's Christmas; Angel
City; Abduction; Poker Alice (CBS)-
1986; mini-series: The Awakening
Land (CBS); *also numerous features*

BASER, Michael
  Agent: Leading Artists
  Tel.: (213) 858-1999

credits:
series: (All co-written with Kim
Weiskopf): 9 to 5 (also produced);
Three's Company (exec. story consultant); Carter Country (exec. story
editor); Good Times (story editor); We
Got It Made (exec. story editor); Automan; What's Happening Now!
(exec.prod.)-1987

BEGEL, Cindy
  Agent: Shapiro-Lichtman
  Tel.: (213) 557-2244

credits:
series: Alice; The New Leave It To
Beaver-1985-86; Together We Stand-
1987

BENCHLEY, Peter
 Agent: Martha Luttrell, ICM
 Tel.: (213) 550-4000

credits:
Barrington (CBS)-1987; *3 features
including Jaws.*

BERK, Michael
 Bus.: BSR Productions
 c/o 20th Century Fox
 10201 W. Pico Blvd.
 Los Angeles, CA 90035
 Tel.: (213) 203-3465

credits:
m.o.w.s: (all with Douglas Schwartz)
The Incredible Journey of Dr. Meg
Laurel; The Ordeal of Dr. Mudd;
Crime of Innocence; Tha Haunting
Passion; series: Manimal; The Wizard
(CBS)-1986-87; *has deal in association
with GTG Entertainment*

BOCHCO, Steven
 office: Twentieth Century
 Fox
 10201 W. Pico Blvd.
 Los Angeles, CA 90035
 Tel.:(213) 277-2211
 Atty: Frank Rohner, Esq.
 Tel.: (213)-274-6182

credits:
Hill Street Blues -1981-1985 (also exec.
Prod.); L.A. Law (also exec. prod.)
1986-87.

BOROWITZ, Andy
 (Also, see Producers)
 Agent: William Morris
 Agency
 Tel.: (213) 274-7451

credits:
Square Pegs; Easy Street (NBC)-1986-
87

BORTMAN, Michael
 Agent: Creative Artists
 Tel.: (213) 277-4545

credits:
Who Will Love My Children-1983;
Single Bars, Single Women-1984

BRENNERT, Alan
 Agent: Joel Gotler
 Tel.: (213) 275-6330

credits:
 The Twilight Zone (multiple
episodes)(CBS)-1986

BROOKS, Hindy
 Agent: Martin Hurwitz,
 ICM
 Tel.: (213) 550-4000

credits:
series: Eight is Enough; Fame-1982;
Lottery-1983-84; Jessie-1984; m.o.w.'s:
The Long Days of Summer; Before and
After (ABC)

writers

BROOKS, James L.
  Bus.: Gracie Films
  20th Century Fox
  10201 W. Pico Blvd
  Los Angeles, CA 90035
  Tel.:(213) 203-3771

credits:
Taxi, Cheers, The Tracy Ullman Show-1987
Features: Terms of Endearment-1984

BULLOCK, Harvey
  Agent: Sylvia Hirsch
  Sy Fischer Company
  Tel.: (213) 969-2900

credits:
series include: Th Andy Griffith Show;
The New Odd Couple; Love Boat; One
Day At a Time; Flo; m.o.w.: Return to
Mayberry (with Everett Greenbaum)
(NBC)-1986

BURNS, Allan
  Agent: John Gaines, A.P.A.
  9000 Sunset Blvd., 12th Fl.
  Los Angeles, CA 90069
  Tel.: (213)273-0744

credits:
series: Get Smart; Love, American
Style; Mary Tyler Moore; Rhoda; Lou
Grant; The Duck Factory; *feature: Just
Between Friends*

BYRNES, James
  Agent: Sylvia Hirsch
  The Sy Fischer Co. Agency
  Tel.: (213) 969-2900

credits:
series: Gunsmoke; Knight Rider;
m.o.w.'s: The Gambler (also pro-
duced); The Gambler II; Wild Times;
The Sacketts; Nowhere to Run; How
The West Was Won; Dead Wrong;
Solitary Man; The Shadow Riders;
Clash of Eagles; The Californians; Gun-
smoke: The Movie; Down the Long
Hill; The Gunfighter-1987

CHARLES, Les
  Agt: Broder-Kurland-Webb
  Tel.: (213)656-9262
  Bus.: Charles-Burrows-Charles
  5555 Melrose Avenue
  Los Angeles, CA 90035
  Tel.: (213)468-5000

credits:
The Mary Tyler Moore Show;
M*A*S*H; Taxi-1980-1983; Cheers
(NBC)-1982-87; The Tortellis (NBC) -
1986-87

CHARLES, Glen
  Agent: Bob Broder
  Tel.:(213) 656-9262
  Bus.: Charles-Burrows-Charles
  5555 Melrose Avenue
  Los Angeles, CA 90035
  Tel.: (213)468-5000

credits:
M*A*S*H; The Mary Tyler Moore
Show; Taxi-1980-1983; Cheers (NBC)-
1982-87; The Tortellis (NBC) -1987

CHESLEY, Howard
  Agent: Robert Stein
  Leading Artists
  Tel.: (213) 858-1999

credits:
series: Maximum Security-1984; Lady Blue-1985; The Equalizer-1986; Hunter-1986

CHETWYND, Lionel
  Agent: Triad Artists
  Tel.: (213) 556-2727

credits:
Miracle On Ice-1980; *feature: The Hanoi Hilton-1987*

CROWE, Chris
  Agent: Bauer Benedek Agency
  9255 Sunset Blvd., Ste. 710
  Los Angeles, CA90069
  Tel.: (213) 275-2421

credits:
series: The Hardy Boys; Dark Room; Alfred Hitchcock Presents-1985; Nightmares

DAWKINS, Johnny
  Agent: Paul J. Heller,
  The Agency
  10351 Santa Monica Blvd.
  Suite 211
  Los Angeles, CA 90025
  Tel.: (213) 551-3000

credits:
The Wave (ABC Afterschool Spec.)-1981; Sharon (CBS)-1982; Skag; Lou Grant;

DONIGER, Walter
  (Also, see Directors)
  Agent: Rick Ray, Triad
  Artists
  10100 Santa Monica Blvd.
  Los Angeles, CA 90067
  Tel.: (213)556-2727

credits:
Kentucky Woman (also dir.)

ELIAS, Michael
  Messages: (213)276—6284
  Office: Warner Bros.
  4000 Warner Blvd.
  Burbank, CA 91522
  Tel.: (818) 954-4370

credits:
Head of the Class (also co-creator with Rich Eustis)-1986-87; *features include The Jerk and Young Doctors in Love.*

ESTRIN, Ken
  Agent: Bob Broder
  Broder-Kurland-Webb
  Agency
  8439 Sunset Blvd. # 402
  Los Angeles, CA 90069
  Tel.: (213) 656-9262

credits:
series: Taxi-1989-83; Cheers-1982-85; Shaping Up-1984; The Tortellis (also co-creator)-1987; The Tracy Ullman Show (FBC)-1987

ESTRIN, Jonathan
  Agent: Lee Rosenberg
  Triad Artists
  Tel.: (213) 5556-2727

credits:
m.o.w.'s: Something So Right-1982;
Between Friends (HBO)-1983; series:
Cagney & Lacey (with Shelley List)-
1987

EUSTIS, Rich
  Agent: Mike Ovitz, CAA
  Tel.: (213) 277-4545

credits:
numerous variety specials including
Dom DeLuise & Friends (ABC)-1986;
Head of the Class (ABC), writer &
series creator-1986; features: Serial-
1979; Young Doctors in Love-1982

FONTANA, Tom
  Agent: Paul Schwartzman,
  ICM
  Office: CBS/MTM Studios
  Tel.: (818) 760-5000

credits:
St. Elsewhere (NBC)- 1982-1987

FRIEDENBERG, Richard
  Agent: Daniel Ostroff
  9200 Sunset Blvd., Suite 402
  Los Angeles, CA 90069
  Tel.: (213) 278-2020

credits:
m.o.w.: Promise-1987

GAY, John
  Agent: Rob Graham, CAA
  Tel: (213) 277-4545

credits:
Hunchback of Notre Dame (CBS
m.o.w.)-1981; Witness for the Prosecu-
tion (CBS m.o.w.)-1982; Fatal Vision
(NBC Mini-series)-1984; Doubletake
(CBS mini-series)-1985; Unlce Tom's
Cabin (Showtime)-19856; Outlaw (CBS
m.o.w.)-1986, Six Against the Rock
(NBC m.o.w.)-1987

GELBART, Larry
  c/o Writers Guild of
  America-West
  8955 Beverly Blvd.
  Los Angeles, CA 90048

credits:
M*A*S*H-1974-81; AfterMASH; United
States-1981; *numerous features includ-
ing Oh God! and Tootsie*

GEOGHAN, Jim

  Agent: David Shapira &
  Associates
  15301 Ventura Blvd. # 345
  Sherman Oaks, CA 91423
  Tel.: (818) 906-0322

credits:
Too Close For Comfort-1982; Facts of
Life-1983; Silver Spoons-1984-1987

GOLDMAN, James
  Agent: Sam Cohn, ICM,
  New York
  Tel.: (212) 556-5600

credits:
Oliver Twist-1982; Anna Karenina
(CBS)-1985; Anatassia-1986; *also, two
features*

GOULD, Heywood
  Agent: Robert Bookman
  Creative Artists Agency
  Tel.: (213) 277-4545

credits:
The Equalizer (CBS); *several features
including The Boys From Brazil*

GREEN, Gerald
  Agent: William Morris,
  New York
  Tel.: (212) 586-5100

credits:
m.o.w.: Wallenberg: A Hero's Story
(NBC)-1984

GREEN, Katherine
  Agent: Leading Artists
  Tel.: (213) 858-1999

credits :
Taxi; Cheers; Newhart

GREEN, Patricia
  Agent: Cindy Turtle
  The Rosen/Turtle Agency
  15010 Ventura Blvd.
  Suite 219
  Sherman Oaks, CA 91403
  Tel.:(818) 907-9891

credits:
ABC Afternnon Special; Better Late
Than Never; Eight is Enough (8 episodes); Shirley; King's Crossing;
American Dream; The Missippi (exec.
story consultant); Scarecrow and Mrs.
King (exec. story consultant); Two
Marriages; Cagney and Lacey (multiple episodes, winner Emmy award-
1985); Cagney and Lacey (as producer,
winner Emmy award-1986); North and
South (20 hour mini-series)-1985. Perry
Mason (m.o.w.)-1987   *Curently
developing series and movies of the
week.*

GREENBAUM, Everett
  Agent: Sylvia Hirsch
  Sy Fischer Co.
  Tel.: (213) 969-2900

credits:
series include: Mr Peepers ; The Real
McCoys; Ensign O'Toole; M*A*S*H;
The Odd Couple; Love Boat; Sanford &
Son; AfterMash; m.o.w.: Return to
Mayberry (with Harvey Bullock)-1986,
*also, numerous features including
Good Neighbor Sam*

GRUSIN, Larry
Agent: William Morris
Tel.: (213) 274-7451

credits:
Garbo Talks (feature)-1984; Between Two Women (ABC m.o.w.)-1986

HANALIS, Blanche
Agent: Sylvia Hirsch
The Sy Fischer Company
Tel.: (213) 969-2900

credits include:
m.o.w.'s: The Silent Garden; A Staute of Liberty; A Home of Your Own; The Eleanor & Lou Gehrig Story; Portrait of a Rebel: The Margaret Sanger Story; The Children of An Lac; Pleasure Palace; Camille; Christmas Eve (NBC)-1986

HANLEY, William
Agent: Leo Bookman
William Morris Agency
Tel.: (213) 274-7451

credits:
m.o.w.'s: Something About Ameilia-1983; Celebrity-1983; Nutcracker: Money, Madness, Murder (min-series)-1986; When The Time Comes-1987

HAUCK, Charlie
Agent: Leading Artists
Tel.: (213) 858-1999

credits:
series: Maude (also produced)-5years); The Associates; Thw Two of Us (also produced); Valerie (also created)-1985

HEINEMANN, Arthur
Agent: Sylvia Hirsch
The Sy Fischer Company
Tel.: (213) 969-2900

credits include:
Backwards: The Riddle of Dyslexia; In His Steps; The Joan Kennedy Story: Victims for Victims; Debonair Dancer; series: Bonanza; Little House on the Prairie (4 years); ABC After School Specials (Emmy award)

HERSKOVITZ, Marshall
Bus. Bedford Falls Productions
Tel.: (213) 280-1103
Agent: Rosalie Swedlin, Creative Artists Agency
Tel.: (213) 277-4545

credits:
Family (ABC)-1977-78, The White Shadow (CBS); Chips (NBC); Special Bulletin (NBC Dramatic Special)(Emmy Award)-1983; Jefferson Mall; Thirty Something (also prod.)(ABC)-1987

HIGGINS, Colin
Agent: Creative Artists Agency
Tel.: (213) 277-4545

credits:
Out On a Limb (ABC mini-series)-1986

ISSACS, David
Agent: Broder-Kurland-Webb Agency
Tel.: (213) 656-9262

credits:
(all co-written with Ken Levine):
Cheers (NBC)-1982-86; Mary (exec.
prod.); The Tortellis (NBC)-1986; Tracy
Ullman Show (FBC)-1987; Volunteers
(feature)-1984

KAMPMANN, Steven
Agent:Robert Stein
Leading Artists
Tel.: (213) 858-1999

credits:
WKRP in Cincinnati (also produced)

KANIN, Fay
Agent: Ron Mardigan
William Morris Agency
Tel.: (213) 274-7451
credits:
m.o.w.'s: Heat of Anger; Tell Me
Where It Hurts (emmy award); Hus-
tling; Friendly Fire (emmy award)-
1979; Heartsounds-1985

KANTER, Hal
Bus. Mgr.: James Harper & Associates
Tel.: (818) 788-8683

selected credits:
AFI Salute to Alfred Hitchcock-1979;
Lucy NBC Special-1982; Beyond Witch
Mountain-1982; 55th Annual Acade-
mey Awards (ABC)-1983; You Can't
Take It With You (series)-1987

KASS, Jerry
Agent: Martha Luttrell, ICM
Tel.: (213) 550-4000

credits:
m.o.w.'s: Queen of the Stardust
Ballroom; My Old Man; The Black Stal-
lion Returns (feature)

KITE, Lesa
Agent: Marty Shapiro
8827 Beverly Blvd.
Los Angeles, CA 90048
Tel.: (213)557-2244

credits:
series: Gimme a Break-1982; Oh,
Madeline-1982; Alice-1983-84; Still the
Beaver-1985; The New Leave it to
Beaver-1985-86; Together We Stand-
1986

KLEIN, Dennis
Agent: Leading Artists
Tel.: (213) 858-1999

credits:
series include: The Odd Couple;
Happy Days; Love, American Style;
Sanford & Son; All In the Family; Mary
Hartman; Buffalo Bill

KUKOFF, Bernie
(also, see producers)
Office: Columbia Pictures TV
Tel.: (818) 954-6000

credits include:
series: Tucker's Witch; Joe & Son's;
Detective School; Different Strokes (co-
creator); Rags to Riches (NBC)-1987;

KUKOFF, continued

m.o.w: Lt. Shuster's Wife; numerous comedy/variety specials; *also, Johnny Dangerously (feature)*

LANE, Brian
  Agent: Robinson-Weintraub-Gross
  8428 Melorse Place # C
  Los Angeles, CA 90069
  Tel.: (213) 653-5802

credits:
m.o.w.'s: Getting Even (NBC); Little Girl Lost (CBS); Brief Interlude;

LAURENCE, Marc
  Bus.: UBU Productions
  5555 Melrose Avenue
  Los Angeles, CA 90038
  Tel.: (213) 468-5737

credits:
Family Ties (also producer)-1984-87

LEESON, Michael
  (also, see Producers)
  Agent: Lee Gabler, CAA
  Tel.: (213) 277-4545
  Office 4151 Prospect Avenue
  Tel.: (213) 557-5883

credits:
The Cosby Show (co-creator); I Married Dora (creator)-1987

LEVIN, Lissa
  Agent: Leading Artists
  Tel.: (213) 858-1999

credits:
series: Who's the Boss-1984; Three's a Crowd-1984; Family Ties; Cheers-1983-84; Double Trouble-1985

LEVINE, Ken
  Agent: Broder-Kurland-Webb
  Tel.: (213) 656-9262

credits:
series: (all with David Issacs): Cheers (NBC)-1982-87; AfterMash; Mary-1985-86; The Totrellis (NBC)-1986; Tracy Ullman Show (FBC)-1987

LINK, William
  Agent: William Haber, CAA
  Tel.: (213) 277-4545

credits:
series: Mannix (created); Columbo (created); m.o.w.'s: (all co-written with Richard Levinson) The Execution of Private Slovik; That Certain Summer; My Sweet Charlie; Crisis At Central High; The Gun; Rehearsal for Murder; Take Your Best Shot; The Guardian (HBO)

LIST, Shelley
  Agent: Lee Rosenberg
  Triad Astists
  Tel.: (213) 556-2727

credits:
And Baby Makes Six (NBC m.o.w.)-1979; Baby Comes Home (m.o.w.)-1980; Something So Right (CBS m.o.w.)-1982; Between Friends (HBO)-1983; Cagney & Lacey (with Jonathan Estrin)-1987

FRIES ENTERTAINMENT INC.

A Full Service Company

FRIES TELEVISION

FRIES DISTRIBUTION

FRIES THEATRICAL

FRIES INTERNATIONAL

FRIES HOME VIDEO

FRIES FIRST RUN

6922 Hollywood Boulevard, Los Angeles, Ca 90028

(213) 466-2266 Telex: 3781675

New York · Chicago · London

LLOYD, David
c/o Writers Guild-West
8955 Beverly Blvd.
Los Angeles, CA 90048

credits:
Bob Newhart; Mary Tyler Moore
(emmy award); Lou Grant-1980; Taxi-
1982; Mr. Smith-1983; Brothers; Mr.
Sunshine-1985; Cheers-1982-85; Amen-
1987

MANKIEWICZ, Tom
Agent: Rand Holsten, CAA
Tel.: (213) 277-4545

credits:
Hart to Hart (m.o.w.)-1979; Hart to
Hart (series)
*has written numerous feature films,
directed* Dragnet 1987.

MANN, Abby
Agent: Jim Wiatt, ICM
Tel.: (213) 550-4000

credits:
Report to the Commissioner-1975;
Medical Center; NBC Best Sellers; The
Atlanta Child Murders (CBS)-1984;
War and Love-1985; Kojak (2hr)-1987

MARKUS, John
Agent: Jim Berkus
Leading Artists, Inc.
Tel.: (213) 658-1999

credits:
Facts of Life-1982; Taxi-1982;
Amanda's-1983; The Cosby Show
(head writer)-1984-86; A Different
World (CBS)-1987

MARTINEZ, Al
Agent: William Morris Agency
Tel.: (213) 274-7451

credits:
series: Hawaii 5-0-1978; The Bad Cats-
1980; Airwolf-1985; m.o.w.'s: Betrayal
of Trust; That Secret Sunday (CBS)-
1986

MASIUS, John
Agent: Paul Schwartzman,ICM
Tel.: (213) 550-4000

credits:
St. Elsewhere (NBC)-1982-87

McGREEVEY, John
Agent: Sylvia Hirsch
The Sy Fischer Company
3330 Cahuenga Blvd., # 300
Los Angeles, Ca 90068
Tel.: (213) 969-2900

credits include:
m.o.w.'s : The Samantha Smith Story;
Consenting Adult; The Secret Smile;
Judge Horton and the Scottsboro Boys;
Pope John XXIII; The Walton's Easter
Story; The Death of Richie; Charles and
Diana; Flight 90; The Best Years of Our
Lives; The Millionaire; Return of
Marcus Welby; A Time to Live; Unholy
Matrimony (CBS)-1987; mini-series:
Roots II-1977; Murder In Texas-1983;
series: The Waltons (Emmy award)

McKEAND, Nigel and Carol
Agent: Bill Haber, CAA
Tel.: (213) 277-4545

credits:
Family (ABC); Alex, the Life of a Child (ABC)-1987

McNEELEY, Jerry
(Also, see Producers)
Office: Lorimar-Telepictures Studios
Tel.: (213) 558-5000

credits include:
Sin Of Innocence (m.o.w.)-1984, Our House (NBC series)-1986-88

MISHKIN, Philip
Agent: Roger Davis
William Morris Agency
Tel.: (213) 274-7451

credits:
m.o.w's: Not Just Another Affair-1982; series: Gimme a Break-1983; Three's a Crow-1984-85; Detective In House-86; Training Camp-1986

MOFFETT, Jordan
Agent: Jim Berkus
Leading Artists, Inc.
445 N. Bedford Drive
Beverly Hills, CA 90210
Tel.: (213) 858-1999

credits:
House Calls; One Day at a Time; Barney Miller; It Takes Two-1983-84; The Duck Factory-1983-84; Detective In House; Spies-1986

MOYE, Michael G.
Agent: Leading Artists
Tel: (213) 858-1999

credits:
series: Good Times; Silver Spoons; The Jeffersons (5 years); It's Your Move; "227"; Married... With Children (also exec. producer)(FBC)-1987

MUMFORD, Thad
Agent: Leading Artists
Tel.: (213) 858-1999

credits:
series: The Electric Company; Maude; Angie; M*A*S*H (4yrs.); The Duck Factory; The Cosby Show-1986; Alf (producer)-1986-87; A Different World (NBC)-1987

NEIGHER, Stephen
Agent: Jim Berkus
Leading Artists, Inc.
Tel.: (213) 858-1999

credits:
The Ropers; Working Stiffs; It Takes Two; The Facts of Life; Barnery Miller; The Jeffersons

NIXON, Agnes

credits:
Guiding Light; Another World; Search For Tomorrow (created & prod.); As the World Turns (created & prod.); øne Life to Live (created & prod.); All My Children (created & prod.).

PARKER, Jim
(also, see Producers)
Agent: Stephanie Rogers & Assoc.
3855 Lankershim Blvd., Suite 218
North Hollywood, CA 91604
Tel.: (818) 509-1010

credits:
series: Love Sidney; Mork & Mindy;
Love, American Style; He and She;
That Girl; Welcome Back Kotter;
Mama's FAmily; Love Boat; Cheers;
Growing Pains; Perfect Strangers-1986;
Amen (CBS)-1987; *also 2 feature films.*

PATCHETT, Tom
Pers. Mgr.: Bernie Brillstein
Tel.: (213) 275-6135

credits include:
series: Open All Night (with Jay
Tarses)-1981; Buffalo Bill (with Jay
Tarses)-1982-83 (NBC); Washingtoon-
1985; Alf (multiple episodes)-1986;
features include The Great Muppet
Caper and The Muppets Take Manhattan

PATIK, Vickie
Agent: William Morris Agency
Tel.: (213) 274-7451

credits:
Do You Remember Love (m.o.w.)
(CBS)-1985

PEYSER, Lois
Agent: Elaine Markson, New York
Tel.: (212) 243-8480

credits:
Dick Van Dyke Show; Love American
Style; The Winners (CBS Special)-1977;
The Violation of Sarah Mc David (CBS
m.o.w.)-1981

PHELAN, Anna Hamilton
Agent: Rosalie Swedlin, CAA
Tel.: (213) 277-4545

credtis:
Mask (feature)-1985; Swallows Come
Back (HBO)-1987

PHILLIPS, Clyde
(also, see Producers)
Bus.: Columbia Pictures TV
Columbia Plaza
Burbank, CA 91505
Tel.: (818) 954-6000

credits:
Trapper John, M.D. (CBS); Midas
Valley (co-creator); Houston Knights
(CBS)(co-writer)-1986-87

RODGERS, Mark
Agent: Frank Cooper
The Cooper Agency
10100 Santa Monica # 310
Los Angeles, CA 90067
Tel.: (213) 277-8422

credits:
series: Ironsides; Kojack; m.o.w.'s:
Police Story II-1977; Masquarade;
Dirty Dozen III-1987; Police Story: The
Freeway Killings -1987

ROSE, Reginald
Agent: Sylvia Hirsch
Sy Fischer Co. Agency
3330 Cahuenga Blvd.
Los Angeles, CA 90068
Tel.: (213) 969-2900

credits:
Dear Friends; Thunder on Sycamore
Street; Tragedy in a Temporary Town;
Two Loves; The Rules of Marriage;
Studs Lonigan; Escape from Sobibor
(CBS)-1987; also, *10 features including
12 Angry Men, The Wild Geese; and
Whose Life Is It, Anyway?*

ROSENBERG, Stuart
Agent: Leading Artists
Tel.: (213) 858-1999

credits:
Nurse; Baker's Dozen; The Cutting
Room (CBS m.o.w.)

RUBEN, Albert
Agent: Sylvia Hirch
The Sy Fischer Co. Agency
Tel.: (213) 969-2900

credits:
series: Have Gun, Will Travel; Streets
of San Francisco; Kojak; The Nurses;
Room 222; m.o.w.'s: The Belarus File;
The Connection; Foster and Laurie;
City In Fear; The French Connection II;
Trackdown; Reunion At Fairborough;
Countdown to Looking Glass

SACKETT, Nancy
Agent: Broder-Kurland-Webb
Tel: (213) 656-9262

credits:
Mulligan Stew -1977; Lou Grant;
Glitter-1982; Fairie Tale Theatre
(Showtime)-1986; m.o.w.'s: Skyward
(NBC)-1980; Where Are My Children
(CBS)-1981; Weekends (ABC); A
Bridge to Terebeithia (PBS)-1984; Bev-
erly Hills Madam-1986; Intimate
Betrayal-1987

SAYLES, John
Agent: Robinson-Weintraub-Gross
8428 Melrose Place # C
Los Angeles, CA 90069
Tel.: (213) 653-5802

credits:
m.o.w.s: A Perfect Match (CBS)-1980;
Unnatural Causes-1986; *also writer
and director of numerous features
including Brother From Another
Planet and Matewan*

SCHNEIDER, Barry
Agent: Sylvia Hirsch
Sy Fischer Co.
3330 Cahuenga Blvd. #300
Los Angeles, CA 90068
Tel.: (213) 969-2900

credits:
Doctor For The Prosecution (CBS); One
Man's Poison (NBC); Badge of Honor
(CBS); Susan Penny Story (NBC);
Secret Passions (NBC)

SCHREINER, William
  Agent: Nancy Roberts
  Tel.: (213) 275-9384
  messages: (818) 994-7251

credits:
Proving Ground-1986; Late Riser
(m.o.w.-upc.)

SEEGER, Susan
  (Also, see Producers)
  Agent: Broder-Kurland-Webb
  Tel.: (213) 656-9262

credits:
Duet (created)-1987

SHAVELSON, Melville
  Agent: Willian Morris Agy.
  Tel.: (213) 274-7451

credits:
Ike (mini-series)-1979; Deceptions
(m.o.w.)-1985

SILLIPHANT, Stirling
  Agent: Bill Haber, CAA
  Tel.: (213) 277-4545

credits:
Space (CBS mini-series)-1985; m.o.w.'s:
Mussolini-the Untold Story-1985; *nu-
merous features*

SLOAN, Michael
  Agent: Jim Wiatt, ICM
  Tel.: (213) 550-4000

credits: Simon & Simon-1982; The
Master-1984; The Equalizer (also

created)-1985; Rivera-1987; m.o.w.'s:
Return of the Man From Uncle-1983;
The Return of the Six Million Dollar
Man and the Bionic Woman-1986

TARSES, Jay
  Per. Mgr.: Bernie Brillstein
  Tel.: (213) 275-6135

credits:
series: Tony Randall Show-1978; Open
All Night-1981; Buffalo Bill (also co-
creator)-1982-84; The Days and Nights
of Molly Dodd (also created) (NBC)-
1987; *features include The Muppets
Take Manhattan (with Tom Patchett)*

TOROKEVEI, Peter
  Agent: Roger Davis
  William Morris Agency
  Tel.: (213) 274-7451

credits:
WKRP; *features include Back to School*

TREVEY, Ken
  Agent: Michael Douroux
  Lake & Douroux
  Tel.: (213) 557-0700

credits:
m.o.w.'s: Amber Waves-1980; A
Stranger in the House-1982; LBJ: The
Early Years (NBC)-1987

WALLACE, Earl W.
  Agent: Robert Stein
  Leading Artists, Inc.
  Tel.: (213) 658-1999

credits:
series: For Love and Honor-1984;
Seven Brides for Seven Brothers;
m.o.w.'s: Dillinger; The Last Ride of
the Dalton Gang; The Wild Women of
Chasity Gulch-1981; War and Remembrance (mini-series); *features include
Witness (Academy Award)*

WEEGE, Reinhold
 Agent: Ben Conway & Assocs.
 999 N. Doheny Drive # 403
 Los Angeles, CA 90069
 Tel.: (213) 271-8133
 Business: Starry Night Productions
 Tel.: (818) 954-6000

credits:
series: Barney Miller-1975-79; Fish;
M*A*S*H; WKRP in Cincinatti; Park
Place-1980-81; Night Court (writer &
creater)-1983-87

WEINBERGER, Ed
 (Also, see Producers)
 Bus.: Carson Productions
 5555 Melorse Avenue
 Los Angeles, CA 90038
 Tel.: (213) 468-5000

credits:
 Taxi; Cheers; The Cosby Show (co-
creator)
President of Carson Productions

WEISKOPF, Kim
 Agent: Leading Artists
 Tel.: (213)858-1999

credits:
(All co-written with Michael Baser); 9
to 5 (also produced); Three's Company; Carter Country; Good Times; We
Got it Made; Automan; What's Happening Now! (exec.producers)-1987

WHELPLEY, John
 Agent: Leading Artists
 Tel.: (213)858-1999

credits:
CBS Children's Special (1 Hr.); Starsky
and Hutch; Vegas; Charlie's Angeles;
Love Boat; Fantasy Island; Trapper
John, M.D. (3 years exec. script con-
sultant); Kay O'Brien, Surgeon-1986

WILCOX, Dan
 Agent: Leading Artists
 Tel.: (213) 858-1999

credits:
mini-series: Roots II; series: Sesame
Street (Emmy Award); M*A*S*H (also
producer); The Duck Factory; Bay City
Blues; Newhart

WOUK, Herman
 Agent:c/o BSW Literary
 Tel.: (212-342-0142

credits:
The Winds of War (ABC mini-series)-
1983; War and Remembrance (ABC
mini-series)-1987

WRYE, Donald
  Agent: John Ptak, William Morris
  Tel.: (213) 274-7451

credits:
m.o.w.'s: Divorce Wars; A Love Story-1982; The Face of Rage-1983; mini-series: Amerika (16 hrs.)(ABC)-1987

YOUNG, Dalene
  Agent: Don Kopaloff
  Tel.: (213) 203-8430
  Office: Embassy Communications

credits:
m.o.w.'s: Will There Be a Morning; Dead Man's Curve; The Freddie Prinze Story; Christmas Coalmine Disaster; Dawn: Portrait of a Teenage Runaway; Marilyn

YOUNG, John Sacret
  Agent: George Diskant Agency
  1033 Gayley Ave.# 202
  Los Angeles, CA 90024
  Tel.: (213) 824-3773

credits:
A Rumor of War (CBS Special m.o.w.);
Testament-1983

ZELLMAN, Shelly
  Agent: Leading Artists,Inc.
  Tel.: (213) 858-1999

credits-series:
Benson; Barney Miller; Three's Company; Newhart -1984-86; Spencer For Hire-1985; m.o.w.'s: Born to Raise Heck (CBS)-1984

ZITO, Stephen
  Agent: Robinson-Weintraub-Gross
  Tel.: (213) 653-5802

credits:
m.o.w.'s: A Gun in the House; I Was a Mail Order Bride; Terror In The Sky (NBC)-1985; series: Kay O'Brien; *features include The Escape Artist.*

ZWEIBEL, Alan
  c/o Writers Guild of America-East
  Office: 4151 Prospect Avenue
  Los Angeles, CA 90046

credits:
Saturday Night Live-1979-1980; Steve Martin's Best Show Ever-1981; The New Show-1984; Big Shots in America-1985; It's Garry Shandling's Show (also co-created)-1986-88; *features include Gilda Live and Dragnet '87*

STUDIO
&
PRODUCTION COMPANY
EXECUTIVES

COLUMBIA/EMBASSY TELEVISON
Columbia Plaza
Burbank, CA 91505
Tel.: (818) 954-6000
(A unit of Coca-Cola Television)

GARY LIEBERTHAL
Chairman & Chief Executive Officer
Columbia/Embassy Television

BARBARA CORDAY
President & Chief Operating Officer,
Columbia/Embassy Television

BARRY THURSTON
President, Syndication

STEVE BERMAN
Executive Vice President, Current
Dramatic Programming & Develop-
ment, Columbia

FRANCIS C. McCONNELL
Executive Vice President, Current
Comedy Programming & Develop-
ment, Embassy

VALERIE CAVANAUGH
Senior Vice President in charge of
Business Affairs

JAN E. ABRAHMS
Senior Vice President, Business Affairs

TIM FLACK
Senior Vice President, Talent & Cast-
ing , Columbia

SEYMOUR FRIEDMAN
Senior Vice President, Production,
Columbia

STEPHEN KOLZAK
Senior Vice President, Talent and
Casting , Embassy

KEN STUMP
Senior Vice President, Production,
Embassy

KEN WERNER
Senior Vice President, Business Affairs

STEVE ASTOR
Vice President , Advertising, Publicuty
& Promotion, Columbia

EDUARDO G. CERVANTES
Vice President, Current Programs,
Embassy

DEBROAH CURTAN
Vice President, Current Programs,
Embassy

DOM DeMESQUITA
Vice President, Corporate Communia-
tions, Embassy

PETER GIAGNI
Vice President, Comedy Development,
Embassy

HELEN HERNANDEZ
Vice Presidnet, Public Relations

ANDREW J. KAPLAN
Vice President

ELLEN LEVINE
*Vice President, Drama Development,
Columbia*

GARY LEVINE
Vice President, Current Programs

LAURIE LEVIT
*Vice President, Movies & Mini-series,
Columbia*

DAVID MUMFORD
Vice President, Research

JEFF OSHEN
*Vice President, Talent & Casting,
Columbia*

AL SIMON
*Vice President, Live & Tape Produc-
tion, Columbia*

SUSAN SIMONS
Vice President, Daytime Programs

LESLIE Z. TOBIN
*Vice President, Syndication, Motion
Picture Sales & Acquisitions*

MICHAEL ZUCKER
Vice President, Marketing

LAURI MAEROV
Director, Current Programming

WALT DISNEY TELEVISON
TOUCHSTONE TELEVISION

500 South Buena Vista Street
Burbank, CA 91521
Tel.: (818) 840-1000

JEFFREY KATZENBERG
Chairman, The W alt Disney Studios

RICHARD FRANK
President, The W alt Disney Studios

JEFFREY ROCHLIS
Senior V ice Pr esident, Finance and Administration

WALT DISNEY PICTURES AND TELEVISION / TOUCHSTONE PICTURES AND TELEVISION

MARTY KATZ
Senior Vice President - Motion Pictures and Television Production

EUGENE C. BROWN
Vice President - Controller

BEN COWITT
Vice President - Studio Operations

TERRENCE R. HUSTEDT
Vice President - Finance

DAVID McCANN
Vice President - Post Productions

CHRIS MONTAN
Vice President - Music

GRETCHEN RENNELL
Vice President - Casting

WALT DISNEY TELEVISION

GARY KRISEL
President - Network Television

GARY BARTON
Senior Vice President - Production / Disney Sunday Movie

BILL KERSTETTER
Senior Vice President - Business and Legal Affairs

GRANT ROSENBERG
Senior Vice President - Network Television Development

MITCH ACKERMAN
Vice President - Television Production

DON DeLINE
Vice President Production - Disney Sunday Movie

89

JOHN HUNCKE
Vice President - Business Affairs

ANTHONY JONAS
Vice President - Network Television Development

DAVID MAYER
Vice President - Legal Counsel

PAM McKISSICK
Vice President - Specials

JOHN REAGAN
Vice President - Business Affairs

MICHAEL WEBSTER
Vice President - Television Animation

LAURIE YOUNGER
Director, Network Television Development

BUENA VISTA TELEVISION

ROBERT JACQUEMIN
Senior Vice President

PETER AFFE
Vice President - Eastern Operations

JAMIE BENNETT
Vice President - Programming and Production

LARRY FRANKENBACH
Vice President - Midwest Division Manager

RICHARD GOLDMAN
Vice President - General Sales Manager

MARY KELLOGG-JOSLYN
Vice President - Programming and Production

MICHAEL MELLON
Vice President - Research

RICHARD NORTH
Vice President - Advertising Sales

DAVID MORRIS
Vice President - Western Division Manager

PETER NEWGARD
Vice President - Southern Division Manager

MICHAEL TANNER
Vice President - Creative Services

MARK ZORADI
Vice President - General Manager

FRIES ENTERTAINMENT, INC.
6922 Hollywood Boulevard
Los Angeles, CA 90028
Tel.: (213) 466-2266

CHARLES W. FRIES
Chairman of the Board

CHARLES M. FRIES
Executive Vice President, Administration

CLIFFORD ALSBERG
Executive Vice President, TV Development

TERRY ALLEN
Vice President, Series Development

THOMAS NUMAN
Vice President, Movies and Miniseries

NICK ARNOLD
In-House Producer for Fries Entertainment

AVE BUTENSKY
Executive Vice President, Domestic Distribution

LARRY FREDERICKS
Executive Vice President, International Distribution, Fries Distribution Company

LOU WEXNER
Vice President, Advertising and Promotions

ALLEN SCHWARTZ
Vice President, First Run Syndication

BRYAN HICKOX
Vice President, Production Supervision

LEN LEVY
Executive Vice President, Fries Home Video

LORIMAR-TELEPICTURES
10202 West Washington Boulevard
Culver City, CA 90230
Tel.: (213) 558-5000

MERV ADELSON
Chairman & Chief Executive Officer

MICHAEL GARIN
Office of the Pr esident

DICK ROBERTSON
Office of the Pr esident

DAVID E. SALZMAN
Office of the Pr esident

MICHAEL J. SOLOMON
Office of the Pr esident

J. ANTHONY YOUNG
*Executive V ice Pr esident & Chief
Financial Officer*

BARBARA S. BROGLIATTI
*Senior Vice President, Worldwide
Corporate Communications*

STEPHEN DAVIDSON
*Senior Vice President, Corporate
Finance*

CAROL J. HENRY
*Senior Vice President, Corporate
Development*

SID MARSHALL
*Senior Vice President, Advertisng
Group*

MICHAEL MELTZER
*Senior Vice President & Group
Controller*

BURTON VAUPEN
Senior Vice President, Administration

LORIMAR TELEVISION

DAVID SALZMAN
President

KEN HORTON
*Senior Vice President, Network
Current Programs*

LESLIE MOONVES
*Senior Vice President, Network
Development*

ROBERT ROSNEBAUM
*Senior Vice President, Network
Production*

BARRY STAGG
*Senior Vice President, Publicity &
Network Promotion & Advertising*

DAVID STANLEY
*Senior Vice President, In Charge of
Business Affairs*

SCOTT STONE
*Senior Vice President, First Run &
Daytime Programming*

JULIE WAXMAN
Senior Vice President, Business Affairs

ANDY ACKERMAN
Vice President, Network Production

ANITA ADDISON
Vice President, Network Dramatic Series Development

ELLEN FRANKLIN
Vice President, Network Comedy Series

WILTON HAFF
Vice President, Business Affairs

SUNTA IZZICUPO
Vice President, Network Movies & Mini-series

MATHEW KNOX
Vice President, Network Post-Production

SANDRA MORRIS
Vice President, Business Affairs

PHIL LARGE
Vice President, Program Services

DEBORAH OPPENHEIMER
Vice President, Network Production

MICHAEL DONHEW
Senior Vice President, Worldwide Product Acquisitions

EDWARD O. DENAULT
Senior Vice President, Lorimar Studios

BARABARA MILLER
Senior Vice President, Talent, Lorimar Productions

JIM McGILLEN
President, Station Sales, Syndication

SCOTT CARLIN
President, First-Run Syndication

KARL KUECHENMEISTER
President, Media Sales

JERRY GOTTLIEB
Chief Executive Officer, Lorimar Home Video

STEVE BORNSTEIN
Senior Vice President, Programming, Home Video

JEFF JENEST
Senior Vice President, Marketing

M. JASON ZELIN
Vice President, Acquisitions

CONGRATULATIONS
PARAMOUNT PICTURES

OUR VERY
BEST WISHES
ON YOUR
75th
ANNIVERSARY

MGM/UA TELEVISION PRODUCTIONS, INC.
10000 West Washington Boulevard
Culver City, California 90232
Tel.: (213) 280-6000

DAVID GERBER
President

LYNN LORING
Executive Vice President

CHRISTOPHER SEITZ
Senior Vice President, Production

MARK PEDOWITZ
Senior Vice President, Business Affairs and Administration

DIANE SOKOLOW
Senior Vice President, Longform

DEE BAKER
Vice President, Videotape Operations

ELLEN ENDO-DIZON
Vice President, Development, Comedy

LESLIE H. FRENDS
Vice President, Administration

DENNIS JUDD II
Vice President, Production

STEVE KNISELY
Vice President, Business Affairs

RON LEVINSON
Vice President, Current Programming

RON MASSARI
Vice President, Syndication Development

JUDY PALNICK
Vice President, Development, Dramatic Series

GEORGE PARIS
Vice President, Syndicated Programs & Special Projects

BRUCE POBJOY
Vice President, Post Production

KIM REED
Vice President, Advertising , Publicity & Promotion

MARY JO SLATER
Vice President, Casting

NEW WORLD TELEVISION GROUP
1440 Sepulveda Boulevard
Los Angeles, CA 90025
Tel.: (213) 444-8100

EDWARD B. GRADINGER
President & Chief Executtive Officer

PETER R. BIERSTEDT
Executive Vice President & General Counsel

ALBERT T. LINTON
Executive Vice President & Chief Financial Officer

NEW WORLD TELEVISION PRODUCTIONS

JON FELTHEIMER
President

FREYDA ROTHSTEIN
Senior Vice President, Creative Affairs

LEA STALMASTER
Vice President of Programs

MICHAEL LEVINE
Vice President, DramaticDevelopment

MARLA GINSBERG
Vice President, Creative Affairs

JIM BEGG
Senior Vice President of Production

MARY-ELLIS BUNIM
Vice President, Tape Programs

LORIN SALOB
Executive In Charge of Production

TODD BAKER
Director of Development

DEBBIE INGRAM
Manager of Comedy Development

ERIC TANNENBAUM
Manager of Creative Affairs

J. B. LYON
Department Coordinator

AL D'OSSCHE
Director of Production & Budgets

JUDY SOLOMON
Director of Producer Services

NWT GROUP BUSINESS & LEGAL AFFAIRS/FINANCE

GEORGE REEVES
Senior Vice President, Business Affairs & Acquisition

PETER KNEPPER
Senior Vice President, Finance

NEIL SHENKER
Vice President, Business Affairs

HONI ALMOND
Vice President, Business Affairs

KAREN MAGID
Vice President, Legal Affairs

DOUG BEATTY
Director of Production Budgets & Business Affairs Administration

NEW WORLD TELEVISION DISTRIBUTION

TONY BROWN
Senior Vice President, General Sales Manager

JAMES McNAMARA
Senior Vice President, International Distribution

DORTHY HAMILTON-CORONA
Director Sales & Service

THEA DISERIO
Manager of International Sales and Promotions

NEW WORLD TELEVISION MARKETING/PUBLICITY/PROMOTION

GLORIA LAMONT
Director of Marketing

JUSTIN PIERCE
Director of Publicity

MARK SHULTE
Manager, National Promotions

NEW WORLD VIDEO

PAUL CULBERG
President & General Sales Manager

ROY COX
Vice President, Acquisitions & Development

RICK GITTLESON
Acquisitions Director

DAVID PIERCE
Vice President of Sales

DENA HOLEY
Vice President, Creative Services

LESLIE O'BRIEN
Vice President, Marketing

EMILY FARR
Vice President, Finance & Operations

PARAMOUNT PICTURES TELEVISION GROUP
5555 Melrose Avenue
Los Angeles, CA 90038
Tel.: (213) 468-5000

MEL HARRIS
President

ROBERT KLINGENSMITH
President, Video

JOHN S. PIKE
President, Network Television

LUCILLE S. SALHANY
President, Domestic Television

STEVEN A. GOLDMAN
Executive Vice President, Sales & Marketing

CECELIA R. ANDREWS
Senior Vice President, Business Affairs-Network TV

HOWARD BARTON
Senior Vice President, Legal Affairs-Network TV

KIRK DODD
Senior Vice President, Business Affairs/Finance-Domestic TV

JEFFREY HAYES
Senior Vice President, Creative Affairs-Network TV

FRANK H. KELLY
Senior Vice President, Programming-Domestic TV

R. GREGORY MEIDEL
Senior Vice President, General Sales Manager

ALAN BAKER
Vice President, Programming, Domestic Television

RICHARD K. BERMAN
Vice President, Longform and Special Projects

HOLLACE BROWB
Vice President, Advertising, Home Video

PAUL J. HELLER
Vice President, Series Development-Network TV

HELEN MOSSLER
Vice President, Talent & Casting-Network TV

STEVEN NALEVANSKY
Vice President, Creative Affairs-Domestic Television

MICHAEL SCHOENBRUN
*Vice President, Production-Network
Television*

JOHN SYMES
*Vice President, Current Programming-
Network TV*

SETH M. WILLENSON
*Vice President, Acquisitions, Develop-
ment-Video*

BARBARA BUCE
Director, Program Development

STEVEN B. GLASSER
Director, Production

CONSTANCE KAPLAN
*Executive Director, Comedy Develop-
ment*

SHARON SAWYER
*Executive Director, Production-
Network Television*

JACK WARTLIEB
*Director, Production, Domestic Televi-
sion*

TRI-STAR TELEVISION
1875 CENTURY PARK EAST
LOS ANGELES, CA 90067
Tel.: (213) 201-2300

VICTOR KAUFMAN
Chairman & Chief Executive Officer
Tri-Star Pictures

SCOTT SIEGLER
President, Television Division

PHYLLIS GLICK
Senior Vice President, Creative Affairs

RANDIS SCHMIDT
Senior Vice President, Legal Affairs

ARNOLD BRUSTIN
Senior Vice President, Business Affairs

HARVEY HARRISON
Vice President, Business Affairs

NEIL MAFFEO
Senior Vice President, Production

RAMONA TEISAN
Vice President, TV Production
Controller

STEVEN MENDELSON
Director, Creative Affairs

TWENTIETH CENTURY FOX TELEVISION

10201 West Pico Boulevard
Los Angeles, CA 90035
Tel.: (213) 277-2211

40 West 57th Street
New York, NY 10019
Tel.; (212) 977-5500

JONATHAN DOLGEN
President, 20th Century Fox T elevision Division

HARRIS L. KATLEMAN
President, Television Production Division

DAVID FREEDMAN
Senior Vice President, TV Business Affairs

CHARLES GOLDSTEIN
Senior Vice President, Production and Finance

DAYNA A. KALINS
Senior Vice President, Current and Dramatic Development

MICHAEL KLEIN
Senior Vice President, Current Comedy and Development

ALAN DUKE
Vice President, Business Affairs

JAMES A. LUSK
Vice President, Post Production

LEE ZUCKERMAN
Vice President, Business Affairs

DOMESTIC DISTRIBUTION

MICHAEL LAMBERT
Executive Vice President, Domestic Syndication

LEONARD J. GROSSI
Senior Vice President, Administration and Operations

BENSON H. BEGUN
Vice President, Business Affairs

JOHN GAROFOLO
Vice President, Creative Services

STEVE LEBLANG
Vice President, Research

JAKE TAUBER
Vice President, First Run Program Development

ALAN WINTERS
Vice President, Administrative and Strategic Planning

UNIVERSAL TELEVISION
100 Universal City Plaza
Universal City, CA 91608
Tel.: (818) 777-1000

KERRY McCLUGGAGE
President

ED MASKET
Senior Vice President, Administration

EARL BELLAMY
Executive Vice President, Production

RICHARD LINDHEIM
Senior Vice President, Programming

CHARMAINE BALLIAN
Vice President, Dramatic Development

JIM KORRIS
Vice President, Dramatic Development

BARBARA ROMAN
Vice President, Comedy Programs

BRAD JOHNSON
Vice President, Comedy Development

TOM THAYER
Vice President, Movies for Television

PETER TERRANOVA
Vice President, Talent, Development and Acquisitions

MARK MALIS
Vice President, TV Casting, Series

ROBERT KELLEY
Vice President, Business Affairs

BURT ASTOR
Vice President, Executive Production Manager

RALPH SARIEGO
Vice President, TV Production

BEN HALPERN
Vice President, Publicity, Promotion & Advertising

WILLIAM J. HAMM
Director of Current Programs

VIACOM ENTERTAINMENT GROUP
VIACOM PRODUCTIONS
10 Universal City Plaza
Universal City, CA 91608
Tel.: (818) 505-7500

VIACOM, INC.

SUMNER REDSTONE
Chairman of the Board

FRANK BIONDI
Chief Executive Officer

WILLARD BLOCK
President, V iacom W orld W ide

PAUL HUGHES
President, Entertainment Gr oup and Broadcast Group

RAUL LEFCOVICH
Sr. Vice President, Viacom World Wide

JOSEPH ZALESKI
President, Domestic Syndication

DENNIS GILLESPIE
Sr. Vice President, Marketing

MICHAEL GERBER
Sr. Vice President

PAUL KALVIN
Sr. Vice President, Sales

RONALD LIGHTHOUSE
Sr. Vice President, Corporate & Legal Affairs

TOBY MARTIN
Vice President, First Run Programming

CHARLE TOLEP
Vice President, Merchandising & Licensing

VIACOM ENTERTAINMENT GROUP

GUS LUCAS
Executive Vice President and President West Coast Operations

BUD GETZLER
Senior Vice President, Consultant

GEORGE FABER
Director of Communications

VIACOM PRODUCTIONS

THOMAS D. TANNENBAUM
President, Viacom Productions

DAVID AUERBACH
Vice President, Drama Development

RICHARD ALBARINO
Vice President, Comedy Development

MIKE MODER
Vice President, Production

ROGER KIRMAN
Vice President, Business Affairs

JAMES SCHWAB
Vice President, Finance

LEO "HAP" WEYMAN
Executive Production Manager

STEVE GORDON
Director of Development, East Coast

NANCY KENDALL McCABE
Director, Drama Development

EMMA TORRES
Director, Comedy Development

BOBBE ANN MOORE
*Director, Current Programming
(Drama) and
Executive Assistant to the President*

KEITH PIERCE
*Director, Current Programming
(Comedy)*

ROBERT GREENFIELD
Director, Business Affairs

HAL HARRISON
Director, Post Production

BILL ROGERS
Director, Business Affairs

BILL BARON
Director of Public Relations

JOHN VASEY
Senior Story Editor

VIACOM NETWORKS GROUP

KENNETH GORMAN
Chairman

JULES HAIMOVITZ
President

JOHN BRADY
Senior Vice President, Finance

GREGORY J. RICCA
Senior Vice President, General Counsel

DWIGHT TIERNEY
Senior Vice President, Administration

VIACOM NETWORK ENTER-PRISES

RON BERNARD
President, Viacom Network Enter-prises

SCOTT KURNIT
President, Viewer's Choice

MADGE RUBENSTEIN
Vice President, Program Acquisition
Viewer's Choice

SARA LEVINSON
Executive Vice President

STEPHAN W. SCHULTE
Executive Vice Pres./General Manager
Viacom Satellite Networks

MATTHEW RIKLIN
Vice President, Business Development

KENYON KRAMER
Director, Program Development
and Production

WARNER BROS. TELEVISION
4000 Warner Blvd.
Burbank, California 91522
Telephone: (818) 954-6000

HARVEY SHEPHARD
President

BARRY MEYER
Executive Vice President

ART STOLNITZ
Senior Vice President, Business Affairs

LARRY LYTTLE
Senior Vice President, Creative Affairs

DOUG DUITSMAN
*Vice President, Senior Advertising,
Publicity & Promotion Executive*

GARY CREDLE
*Vice President, Senior Executive in
Charge of Production*

NORMAN STEPHENS
Vice President, Drama Series Development

ELLY SIDEL
*Vice President, Movies & Miniseries
Development*

DAVID SACKS
Vice President, Current Programming

RON TAYLOR
Vice President, Drama Development

SCOTT KAUFER
Vice President, Comedy Development

PHYLISS HUFFMAN
Vice President, Talent & Casting

BEVERLY NIX
Vice President, Business Affairs

MILT SEGAL
Vice President, Legal Affairs

STEVE PAPAZIAN
Vice President, Film and Tape Production

KAREN PINGITORE
Vice President, Post Production

ART HORAN
Vice President, Business Affairs

TOM TRELOGGEN
*Vice President, Production and
Operations*

ELAINE COHEN
Director, Programming East Coast

GUS BLACKMON
Director, Story & Program Administration

ROSALEE JEFFRIES
Director, Financial Administration

JOE REILLY
Vice President, Business Affairs

MIKE Mc KNIGHT
Director, TV Estimating

KAREN COOPER
Vice President, Special Projects

BOB MACKEY,
Vice President, Legal Affairs

DAVID HIMELFARB
Director, Series Development

MAJOR PRODUCTION
COMPANIES
AND
PRODUCERS

ALLIANCE ENTERTAINMENT
11340 W. Olympic Blvd., Ste.100
Los Angeles, CA 90064
Tel.: (213) 477-5112

David Ginsberg-Chairman
Robert Cooper-Television
John Kemeny-Feature Films
Tom Patricia-Vice President,
  Television Development

THE CANNELL STUDIOS
7083 Hollywood Boulevard
Hollywood, CA 90028
Tel.: (213) 465-5800

Stephen J. Cannell-Chairman,
  Chief Executive Officer
Michael J. Dubelko-President
Jo Swerling, Jr.-Senior Vice
President
Howard D. Kurtzman-Vice
  President, Business & Legal
Affairs
Joseph C. Kaczorowski-Vice
  President, Finance & Admini-
stration

Stephen J. Cannell Prods., Inc.

Peter Roth-President
Matthew N. Herman-Executive
  Vice President
Gary Winter-Vice President,
  Post Production

Lillah McCarthy-Vice President,
  Creative Affairs
Lisa Lewinson-Vice President,
  Publicity, Advertising &
  Promotion
Diane Mandell-Vice President,
  Merchandising & Licensing
Peggy Christianson-Vice Presi-
  dent, Movies & Mini-series for
  Television
Simon Ayer-Director, Talent
Stephen L. Brain-Director,
  Studio Operations
Cindy L. Hauser-Director,
  Public Relations
Joan Etchells-Director,
  Production Administration

CARSON PRODUCTIONS
10045 Riverside Drive
Toluca Lake, CA 91602
Tel.: (818) 506-5333
Production offices:
Paramount Pictures
Tel.: (213) 468-5000

Ed Weinberger-President
David W. Tebet-Executive
  Vice President
Steve Mathes-President of
  Marketing and Distribution

James M. Baldwin-Vice Pres.
of Business Affairs
Arnold Glassberg-Chief Financial Officer
Paul Waigner-Vice President
of Production
Jim Thebaut-Vice President
of Dramatic Development
Helen Sanders-Director of
Administration

dick clark productions
3003 W. Olive Avenue
Burbank, CA 91510
Tel.: (818) 841-3003

Dick Clark-Chairman,
Chief Executive Officer
Francis La Maina-President,
Chief Operating Officer
Ken Ferguson- Chief Financial
Officer
Karen Clark-Vice President,
Administration
Barry Adelman-Vice President,
Television Development
Richard A. Clark-Producer
Lisa Demberg-Vice President,
Creative Affairs
Larry Klein-Producer
Dan Paulson-Vice President,
Movies and Series
Al Schwartz-Vice President,
Productions
Bruce Sterten-Vice President,
Game Show Development
Gene Weed-Vice President,
Television
Martin Weisberg, Esq.
Secretary
Michael Tenzer-Vice President,
Business Affairs
Richard Levine-Vice president,
Programming & Sales
Bryan Thompson-Controller
Tom Stepanchak-Director of
Publicity

COCA-COLA TELECOMMU-NICATIONS
A unit of Coca-Cola-Television
2901 W. Alameda Blvd.
Burbank, CA 91521
Tel.: (818) 954-6000

Herman Rush-Chairman and
Chief Executive Officer
Peter S. Sealey-President and
Chief Operating Officer
Anthony J. Lynn-President,
Cable, Pay Television & Home
Video
Michael Grossman-Executive
Vice President
Philip S. Press-Vice President,
First Run Syndication

COCA-COLA Telecommunications continued

Lance B. Taylor-Vice president,
  Creative Affairs
Paul Coss-Vice President,
  Program Development
June Burakoff-Smith-Vice Pres.,
  Advertising, Publicity, Promotion
Thomas Tardio-Vice President,
  Strategic Planning
Claire Lee-Director, Publicity
  Affairs & Administration
Cynthia Lieberman-Director,
  Advertising & Promotion
Catherine Millard-Manager,
  Audience Promotion
Joe Abrams-Director, First Run
  and Pay Cable

MICHAEL DOUGLAS TELEVISION
10 Universal City Plaza, 32nd fl.
Universal City, CA 91608
Tel.:(818) 505-7589

Michael Douglas-Chairman
C.Z. Wick-President
Susan Braudy-Vice President
Michelle Metzger-Manager of
  Development
Karen Makoff Silby-Assistant
  to the President

GAYLORD PRODUCTION COMPANY
9255 Sunset Blvd.
Los Angeles, CA 90069
Tel.: (213) 271-2193

Ed Gaylord-Chairman
Alan Courtney-President
Peter Alex-Exec. Vice Pres.
  of Development
James Mahoney, Jr.-Vice
  Pres. of TV Development
Bill Banowsky-Pres.
  Gaylord Boradcasting Co.

MERV GRIFFIN ENTERPRISES
1541 N. Vine Street
Hollywood, CA 90028
Tel.: (213) 461-4701

Merv Griffin-Chairman and
  Chief Executive Officer
Bob Murphy-President,
  Chief Operating Officer
Peter Barsocchini-Vice Pres.,
  Motion Picture & films for Tel.
Ray Sneath-Vice President,
  Game Shows and Variety

GROUP W PRODUCTIONS
3801 Barham Blvd. # 200
Los Angeles, CA 90068
Tel.: (213) 850-3800

Edward T. Vane-President &
  Chief Executive Officer
George Resing, Jr.-Senior Vice
  President
Kevin Tannehill-Vice President,
  Sales & Marketing
Meryl Marshall-Vice President,
  Program Affairs
Owen Fimon-Vice President,
  Creative Services

GTG ENTERTAINMENT
The Culver Studios
9336 W. Washington Blvd.
Culver City, CA 90230
Tel.: (213) 836-5537

Grant Tinker-President
Stuart Erwin-Executive Vice
  President
Jay Sandrich-Senior Vice Pres.
Richard Katz-Vice President,
  Business Affairs
Jack Clements-Vice President,
  Production
Steve Friedman-President,
  Program Development Div.

GUBER-PETERS ENTER-TAINMENT CO.
4000 Warner Boulevard
Burbank, CA 91522
Tel.: (818) 954-3517

Peter Guber-Chairman
John Peters-Co-chairman
Stan Brooks-Senior Vice Pres.,
  Television
Jeff Eckeles-director of Develop-
  ment

HARMONY GOLD
8831 Sunset Boulevard #300
Los Angeles, CA 90069
Tel.: (213) 652-8720

Frank Agrama-President &
  Chief Executive Officer
Jehan Agrama-Exec. Vice Pres.
  & Chief Operating Officer
James Mitchell-Chief Financial
  Officer
Heidi Wall-Vice President of
  Programming
Norman Siderow-Vice Pres.
  of Development

INDIEPROD TELEVISION
4000 Warner Blvd
Burbank, CA 91505
Tel.: (818) 954-2600

Daniel Melnick-Chairman
Bruce J. Salan-President
Courtney Pledger-Vice President

INTERSCOPE COMMUNICATIONS
10900 Wilshire Boulevard,
Ste.1400
Los Angeles, CA 90024
Tel.: (213) 208-8525

Frederick W. Field-Chairman
Patricia Clifford-President,
  Television Group
Katie Wright-Vice President
Barbara Gunning-Vice Pres.,
  Development

ITC PRODUCTIONS, INC.
12711 Ventura Blvd.
Studio City, CA 91604
Tel.:(818)760-2110

Jerry Leider-President
Dennis Brown-Executive Vice
  President in charge of Production

Wm. Christopher Gorog-
  Executive Vice President,
  Business Affairs
Glenda Grant-Vice President,
  Television Development
Renee Palyo-Vice President,
  Television Movies and Mini-
  series
Carol Lampman-Director of
  Featur Development
Wendy Pratt-Director
  of Series Development
Susan Leh-Director,
  Publicity
Tim Meyers-Director,
  Post Production
Ted Alben-Manager,
  Television Developmnet
Vince Cheung-Manager,
  Television Movies and Mini-
  series
Harriet Greenberg-Manager,
  Administration and Personnel
Michele P. Schultz-Manager
  of Legal Affairs
Deborah Service-Manager
  of Television Development

LCA/HIGHGATE PICTURES
16 West 61st Street
New York, NY 10023
Tel.: (212) 307-0202

Steve Maier-President
Helen Verno-Sr. Vice President
Frank Doelger-Vice President
Jayne Pliner-Director of
  Literary Affairs

MOTOWN PRODUCTIONS
6255 Sunset Boulevard
Los Angeles, CA 90028
Tel.: (213) 461-9954

Suzanne de Passe-President
Michael Weisbarth-Executive
  Vice President, TV
Carol A. Caruso-Senior Vice
  President-Production
Suzanne Coston-Vice President,
  Musical Features/TV & Stage
Burl A. Hechtman-Vice President
  First Run Syndication and
Home
  Entertainment Programming
Brenda Antin-Director of Creative
  Affairs-West Coast
Laurie Maerov-Director of
Development

Cheryl Hill-Director of Creative
  Affairs-East Coast
Brenda Marzett-Executive
  assistant

MTM
CBS/MTM STUDIOS
4024 Radford Avenue
Studio City, CA 91604
Tel.: (818)760-5000

Arthur Price-President
Mel Blumenthal-Sr. Executive
  Vice President
Tom Palmieri-Executive Vice
  President
Peter Grad-President, Television
Marianne Moloney, President
  MTM Motion Pictures
Joe Indelli- President
  MTM Distribution
Ken Meyer- Executive Vice
Pres.,
  General Counsel
Bill Allen-Senior Vice President,
  Creative Affairs
Geri Windsor-Senior Vice Pres.,
  Talent
Laurence Bloustein-Senior Vice
  Pres., Public Relations
Patricia Ahmann-Vice Pres.,
  Business Affairs

MTM continued

Jim Goodman-Vice President,
  Business Affairs, Labor
Bernie Oseransky-Vice President,
  Production
Ted Rich-Vice President,
  Post Production
Eugene Blythe-Director,
  Television Casting
Lynn Deegan-Vice President,
  Comedy Development
Lynn Dittrick-Director,
  Business Affairs
Mary Jo Ballerini-Director,
Personnel
  and Administration
Eillen Kurtz-Director, Public
  Relations

ORION TELEVISION
1888 Century Park East
6th Floor
Los Angeles, CA 90067
Tel.: (213) 282-0550

Richard Rosenbloom-President
Gary Randall-Senior Vice President
Jeff Wachtel-Vice President
  of Development
Ann Stich-Vice President,
  Current Programming

Nick McAffee-Vice President
  of Post Production
Scott Towle-President of
  Syndication
Robert Oswaks-Sr. Vice Pres.,
  Advertising & Publicity

PARAMOUNT PICTURES TELEVISION GROUP
5555 Melrose Avenue
Los Angeles, CA 90038
Tel.: (213) 468-5000

Mel Harris-President
Robert Klingensmith- Pres.,
Video
John S. Pike-President,
  Network Television
Lucille S. Salhany- President,
  Domestic Television
Steven A. Goldman-Executive
V.P.,
  Sales & Marketing
Cecelia R. Andrews-Senior V.P.,
  Business Affairs-Network TV
Howard Barton-Senior V.P.,
  Legal Affairs-Network TV
Kirk Dodd-Sr. V.P., Business
  Affairs/Finance-Domestic TV
Jeffrey Hayes-Sr.V.P., Creative
  Affairs-Network Television
Frank H. Kelly-Sr. V.P.,
  Programming-Domestic TV

R. Gregory Meidel-Sr.V.P.,
  Gen. Sales Manager
Alan Baker-V.P., Programming
  Domestic Television
Richard K. Berman-V.P.,
  Longform and Special Projects
Hollace Brown-V.P. Advertis-
  ing, Home Video
Meryl Cohen-V.P. Advertising
  and Promotion
Gerald Goldman-V.P., Finance
Howard Green-V.P.,
  Administration-Domestic TV
Paul J. Heller-Vice Pres.,
  Series Development-Network
Ronald J. Jacobson-V.P.
  Business Affairs-Network TV
Thomas F. Mazza-V.P., Research
Helen Mossler-V.P., Talent
  & Casting-Network TV
Steven Nalevansky-V.P.,
  Creative Affairs-Domestic
  Television
Michael Schoenbrun-V.P.
  Production-Network Televi-
sion
John Symes-V.P., Current Prog-
  ramming-Network Telvision
Vance S. VAn Petten-V.P. Busi-
ness & Legal Affairs
Seth M. Willenson-V.P., Acquisi-
tions, Development-Video
Amy Betram-Director,
  Press & Publicity

Barbara Buce-Director, Program
  Development-Domestic TV
Steven B. Glasser-Director,
  Production
Constance Kaplan-Executive
Director, Comedy Development
Helen Ricketts-Executive
  Director, Special Projects
Sharon Sawyer-Executive Dir.,
  Production-Network Televi-
sion
Sondra Scerca-Director, Acqui-
  sistions & Development-Video
Jack Wartlieb-Director,
  Production, Domestic Televi-
sion
John A. Wentworth-Director
  Advertising/Pub./Promotion

PHOENIX ENTERTAINMENT GROUP
310 S. San Vicente Blvd. # 300
Los Angeles, CA 90048
Tel: (213) 657-7502

Gerald I. Isenberg-Co-chairman
Gerald Abrams-Co-chairman
Judy Polone-President
Dick Ravin-Vice President
Marvin Katz-Sr. Vice Pres.
  Business Affairs & Admin.
Barbara Black-Vice President
  of Production

Laura Gibbons-Manager,
Creative Services
Elaine Elfand-Jaeger-Head of
Office Admininistration &
Assistant to the chairman
Marci Forst-Executive Assistant

POUND RIDGE
PRODUCTIONS, LTD.
The Burbank Studios
Producers 6, Suite C
Burbank, CA 91505
Tel.: (818) 954-3371

Irwin Meyer -Co-Chairman &
CEO
Stephen R. Friedman-Co-Chair-
man & CEO
Rodney Sheldon-President
Delores Costello-Administration

PROCTOR & GAMBLE
PRODUCTIONS
9200 Sunset Blvd., Ste, 525
Los Angeles, CA 90069
Tel.: (213) 278-8528

Jack Wishard-Vice President
John K. Potter-Executive in
Charge of Production
Lurie A. Dubrow-Director of
Development
Doni Nelson-Director of Devel-
opment

MARIAN REES ASSOCIATES,
INC.
4125 Radford Avenue
Studio City, CA 91604
Tel.: (818) 508-5599

Marian Rees-President
Ann Hopkins-Vice President,
Development
Bob Huddleston-Executive In
Charge of Production/Pro-
ducer
Gene Miller-Production
Accountant
Kate Forte-Assistant to
the Vice President
Richard Hoffman-Assistant
to Marian Rees

REEVES ENTERTAINMENT
GROUP
3500 W. Olive Ave. # 500
Burbank, CA 91505
Tel.: (818) 953-7600

Richard Reisberg-President
Valerie Cavanaugh-Sr. Vice
President
Jim Landis-Vice Pres., Interna-
tional
Victoria Trauble-Vice Pres.,
Business Affairs

REPUBLIC PICTURES CORP.
12636 Beatrice Street
P.O. Box 66930
Los Angeles, CA 90066
Tel.: (213) 306-4040

Russell Goldsmith-Chairman
  and Chief Executive Officer
Steven Beekes-Vice President
Chuck Larsen-President of
  Domestic Television Distrib.
Joe Levinsohn-Vice President,
  International Sales
Vallery Kountze-Vice President,
  Marketing
Lisa Friedman Bloch-Executive,
  Television Development
Leigh Breechem-Vice President
Sydney Levine-Vice President,
  Video Acquisitions
Preston Fisher-Executive
  Producer
Karen Mack-Executive Producer

**FRED SILVERMAN
COMPANY**
12400 Wilshire Blvd.
Los Angeles, CA 90025
Tel.: (213) 826-6050

Fred Silverman-President
Gigi Levangie-Director of
  Development

**AARON SPELLING
PRODUCTIONS**
Warner Hollywood Studios
1041 N. Formosa Ave.
Los Angeles, CA 90048
Tel.: (213) 850-2500

Aaron Spelling-Chief Executive
  Officer & Chairman
Douglas S. Cramer-
  Executive Vice President
E. Duke Vincent-Senior
  Vice President
Salvatore J. Iannucci-Sr. Vice
  President of Operations and
  Administration
Esther Shapiro-Senior Vice
  President, Creative and
  Corporate Affairs
James A. Roach-Vice Pres.,
  Finance, Treasurer
Norman Henry-Vice Pres.,
  Production
Alan Greisman-Vice Pres.,
  Motion Pictures
Renate Kramer-Vice Pres.
  and Secretary
Arthur Frankel-Vice Pres.
  Business & Legal Affairs
John Nicolaides-Vice Pres.,
  Production Accounting
Joe Dervin-Vice Pres.,
  Post-production
John Woodcock-Supervising
  Film Editor

AARON SPELLING
continued

Ilene Chaiken-Vice President,
  Television Development
Marcia Basichis-Director,
  Current Programming
Susan Zachary-Director of
  Feature Development
Howard Goldin-Manager
  of Development

STONEHENGE
PRODUCTIONS
c/o Paramount Pictures
5555 Melrose Avenue
Los Angeles, CA 90038
Tel.: (213) 468-5000

Dick Berg-President
Allan Marcel-Vice President
Tony Lawless-Director of Devel-
opment
Lauren Weber-Executive Assis-
tant

TAFT ENTERTAINMENT
TELEVISION
10960 Wilshire Blvd.
Los Angeles, CA 90024
Tel.: (213) 969-2800

Neil A. Sterns-Sr. Vice President
  of Program Development
Ellen Glick-Vice President of
  Program Development
Tammy Norman-Manager of
  Program Development

TRI-STAR TELEVISION
1875 Century Park East
Los Angeles, CA 90067
Tel.: (213) 201-2300

Scott Siegler-President
Phyllis-Glick-Senior Vice Pres.,
  Creative Affairs
Neil T. Maffeo-Senior Vice Pres.,
  Production
Susan Finesman Israelson,
  Creative Affairs Exec., East
Coast
Steven Mendelson-Manager,
  Development

VON ZERNECK/SAMUELS PRODUCTIONS
12001 Ventura Place, Suite 400
Studio City, CA 91604
Tel.: (818) 766-2610

Frank von Zerneck
Stu Samuels
Robert Sertner

WEINTRAUB ENTERTAINMENT GROUP
11111 Santa Monica Blvd.,
20th Fl.
W. Los Angeles, CA 90025
Tel.: (213) 312-0776

Jerry Weintraub-Chairman
Andrew Susskind-President
Michael Ross-Vice President,
  Business Affairs
Tom Nunan-Vice President,
  Dramatic Programs
Richard Pierson-Director of
  Comedy Development

DAVID L. WOLPER PRODUCTIONS
4000 Warner Boulevard
Burbank, CA 91522
Tel.: (213) 954-6000

David L. Wolper-President
Auriel Sanderson-Vice President
Mark Wolper-Vice President

THE ZANUCK/BROWN COMPANY
202 N. Canon Drive
Beverly Hills, CA 90210
Tel.: (213) 274-0261

Richard Zanuck
David Brown
Lili Fini Zanuck
Martin Hurwitz
Pamerla Hedley
Lucy Ballantine

TELEVISION NETWORKS

CAP ITAL CITIES/ABC, INC.
ABC ENTERTAINMENT

1330 Avenue of the Americas
New York, NY 10019
Tel.: (212) 887-7777

2020 Avenue of the Stars
Los Angeles, CA 90067
Tel.: (213) 557-7777

THOMAS MURPHEY
Chairman and Chief Executive Officer,
CapCities/ABC, Inc.

DANIEL B. BURKE
President & Chief Operating Officer

MICHAEL P. MALLARDI
President, Broadcasting Group &
Senior Vice President, CapCities/ABC

PHILLIP J. MEEK
President, Publishing Division and
Senior Vice Pres.

JAMES E. DUFFY
President, Communications, Network
and Broadcasting Groups and Vice
President, CapCities/ABC

ROONE ARLEDGE
Group President, ABC News and
Sports

MARK MANDALA
President, ABC TV Network

ABC ENTERTAINMENT-WEST
COAST

BRANDON STODDARD
President, ABC Entertainment

JOHN BARBER
Vice President, Current Series Pro-
grams

STUART BLOOMBERG
Vice President, Comedy and Variety
Series Development

STUART BROWER
Vice President, Creative Services, On-
Air Promotion

TED BUTCHER
Vice President, Film Production, ABC
Circle Films

JOHN CROSBY
Vice President, Casting

CANDACE FARRELL
Vice President, Casting

JOHN HAMLIN
Vice President, Special Programs

TED HARBERT
Vice President, Motion Pictures

EDGAR HIRST
Vice President, Tape Production

CHAD HOFFMAN
Vice President, Dramatic Series
Development

HERB JELLINEK
Vice President in Charge of Production

GEORGE KERAMIDAS
Vice President, Program Planning and Scheduling

DEIRDRE A. PAULINO
Vice President, Administration and Assistant to the President

GARY L. PUDNEY
Vice President and Senior Executive in Charge of Specials and Talent

CHRISTY WELKER
Vice President, ABC Novels for TV and Limited Series

WALLY WELTMAN
Vice President, Daytime Programs

MARK ZAKARIN
Vice President, Creative Advertising

ERIC BELCHER
Director, Advertising and Promotion

CYNTHIA BELL
Director, Current Series Programs

TODD BERGESEN
Director, Comedy Series Development

DENNIS BURGESS
Director, Current Series Programs

DONALD COLHOUR
Director, Special Projects

KIM FLEARY
Director, Comedy Series Development

DOTTIE GAGLIANO
Director, Artist Relations

JILL GREEN
Director, Advertising Services

HANK MILLER
Director, Program Administration

PAULINE MILLER
Director, Current Series Programs

LAUNA NEWMAN-MINSON
Director, Special Programs

ABC ENTERTAINMENT-EAST COAST

MARK H. COHEN
Executive Vice President

PHILIP R. BEUTH
Vice President, Early Morning Programs

JO ANN EMMERICH
Vice President, Daytime Programs

SQUIRE D. RUSHNELL
Vice President, Longe Range Planning and Children's Programs

AMY KOPELAN
Director, Early Morning Programs

RANDI LE WINTER
Director, Daytime Programs

LISA MIONIE
Director, Casting

DELORES MORRIS
Director, Children's Programs

ELEANOR TIMBERMAN
Director, Daytime Program Development

ABC TELEVISION NETWORK GROUP

JOHN B. SIAS
President

JAKE KEEVER
Executive Vice President

GEORGE M. NEWI
Senior Vice President, Affiliate Relations

WARREN D. SCHAUB
Senior Vice President, Finance

MARK ROTH
Vice President, Operations

RICHARD CONNELLY
Vice President, Public Relations

BOB WRIGHT
Vice President, Public Relations, West Coast

CAROL GREENBERG
Director, Series Publicity

JERRY HELLARD
Director, Broadcast Publicity

ABC BUSINESS AFFAIRS WEST COAST

RONALD B. SUNDERLAND
Senior Vice President, Business Affairs and Contracts

BARRY GORDON
Vice President

AL KAPLAN
Vice President, Business Affairs and Contracts

PAT THOMPSON
Director, Business Affairs

126

CBS INC./CBS ENTERTAINMENT

7800 Beverly Boulevard
Los Angeles, CA 90036
Tel.: (213) 852-2345

51 West 52nd Street
New York, NY 10019
Tel.: (212) 975-4321

WILLIAM PALEY
Chairman, CBS Inc.

LAURENCE A. TISCH
President and Chief Executive Officer

CBS BROADCAST GROUP

GENE F. JANKOWSKI
President, CBS Broadcast Group

B. DONDLAD GRANT
President, CBS Entertainment

ROBERT L. HOSKING
President, CBS Radio

THOMAS F. LEAHY
President, CBS Television Network

ERIC OBER
President, CBS Television Stations

NEAL H. PILSON
President, CBS Sports

HOWARD STRINGER
President, CBS News

GEORGE F. SCHWEITZER
Vice President Communications &
Information

CBS ENTERTAINMENT
HOLLYWOOD

B. DONALD GRANT
President, CBS Entertainment

EARLE H. MASTERS III
Vice President, Programs

PAULA BARCELLONA
Vice President, Media Services

TONY BARR
Vice President, CBS Entertainment
Productions

NANCY BEIN
Vice President, Motion Pictures for TV

GEORGE BERNTSON
Vice President, Feature Films and Late-
night Programs

LAYNE BRITTON
Vice President, Business Affairs, West
Coast

MICHAEL S. BROCKTON
Vice President, Daytime, Children's
and Late-night Programs

CASEY MAXWELL CLAIR
Vice President Print Advertising, West
Coast

Pat Faulstich
Vice President, Dramatic Program Development

Peter Frankovich
Vice Presaident, Miniseries

Lisa Freiberger
Vice President, Talent & Casting

Jerold Goldberg
Vice President, On-air Promotion

Herb Gross
Vice President, Planning and Current Programs

Harry Heitzer
Vice President, Business Affairs, Music Operations

William B. Klein
Vice President, Business Affairs

Sid Lyons
Vice President, Business Affairs, Contract Negotiations

Gregg Mayday
Vice President, Comedy Development

James F. McGowan
Vice President, Business Affairs, Administration

Steve Mills
Vice President, Motion Pictures For TV, Miniseries

Norman S. Powell
Vice President, Production Operations

Judy Price
Vice President, Children's Programs & Daytime Specials

Fred Rappoport
Vice President Variety & Informational Specials

Charles Schnebel
Vice President, Current Programs

Robert Silberling
Vice President, CBS Entertainment Motion Pictures for TV

Kit Anderson
Director, Miniseries

Harry B. Chandler
Director, Motion Pictures for TV

Joe Bowen
Director, Primetime Feature Films

Jill Bowman
Director, Variety & Informational Specials

Kathleen Culleton
Director, Administration for Advertising & Promotion

Christopher Gorman
Director , Casting

Maddy Horne
Director, Dramatic Program Development

Barbara Hunter
Director, Daytime Progromming   Carole

Carole M. Kirschner
Director, Comedy Program Development

Brenda Miao
Director, Motion Pictures for TV

Holly Powell
Director, Casting

Renee Rousselot
Director, Casting

Lauren Joy Sand
Director, Dramatic Specials

Larry Strichman
Director, Motion Pictures for TV

Bill Wells
Director, Motion Pictures for TV

CBS BROADCAST GROUP
HOLLYWOOD

Carol A. Alteiri
Vice President, Program Practices

Arnold Becker
Vice President, National TV Research

Charles Cappelman
Vice President Operations, Television City

Ann Morfogen
Vice President, Media Relations, West Coast

CBS ENTERTAINMENT
NEW YORK

Roseanne Leto
Vice President, Programs, New York

John Matoian
Vice President, Program Development

Laurence A. Caso
Vice President, Daytime Programs

Rick Jacobs
Vice President, Talent & Casting

Carolyn Ceslik
Director, Children's Programs

Michael Marden
Director, P rogram Development

Laura Marino
Director, Daytime Casting

FOX BROADCASTING COMPANY
10201 W. Pico Boulevard
Los Angeles, CA 90035
Tel.: (213) 277-2211

BARRY DILLER
Chairman and Chief Executive Officer,
Fox Inc.

JAMIE KELLNER
President and Chief Operating Officer

DAVID JOHNSON
Senior Vice President, Marketing

BRENDA FARRIER
Senior Vice President, Advertising/
Publicity/Promotion

TOM ALLEN
Senior Vice President, Finance &
Administration

ANDY FESSEL
Vice President, Research

BOB MARIANO
Vice President, Affiliate Relations

DAVID FERRARA
Vice President, Affiliate Relations,
Western Region

SCOTT SASSA
Vice President, Network Manage-
ment

PAUL SLAGLE
Vice President, Western Sales

BRAD TURELL
Vice President, Publicity

RON VANDOR
Vice President, Advertising

MICHAEL BINKOW
Vice President, Corporate
Communications, Fox Inc.

PROGRAMMING DIVISION

GARTH ANCIER
Senior Vice President, Programming

JESS WITTENBERG
Senior Vice President, Business Affairs

KEVIN WENDLE
Vice President, Primetime and Late-
night Programming

CHARLES HIRSCHHORN
Vice President, Primetime Develop-
ment

MICHAEL LANSBURY
Director of Series Programming

NBC INC.
NBC ENTERTAINMENT
3000 West Alameda Avenue
Burbank, CA 91523
Tel.: (818) 840-4444

30 Rockefeller Plaza
New York, NY 10112
Tel.: (212) 664-4444

JOHN F. WELCH, JR.
Chairman of the Board

ROBERT C. WRIGHT
*President and Chief Executive Officer,
NBC Inc.*

NBC ENTERTAINMENT

BRANDON TARTIKOFF
President

WARREN LITTLEFIELD
*Senior Vice President, Series, Specials
and Variety Programs*

LEE CURRLIN
*Senior Vice President, East Coast
Programs and Program Planning*

SUSAN BAERWALD
*Vice President, Miniseries and Novels
for TV*

MICHELE BRUSTIN
Vice President, Comedy Programs

JOSEPH CICERO
Vice President, Finance and Administration

IVAN FECAN
*Vice President, Creative Affairs, NBC
Productions*

BRIAN FRONS
Vice President, Daytime Programs

SUSAN LEE
Vice President, Daytine Drama

DON LOUGHERY III
Senior Vice President, NBC Productions

RICHARD LUDWIN
*Vice President, Specials and Variety
Programs*

PERRY MASSEY, JR.
Vice President, Program Production

ANTHONY MASUCCI
Vice President, Motion Pictures for TV

132

LORI OPENDEN
Vice President, Casting

TIM QUEALY
Vice President, Entertainment Productions

PERRY SIMON
Vice President, Drama Productions

ALAN STERNFELD
Vice President, Program Planning

JOEL THURM
Vice President, Talent

PHYLLIS TUCKER VINSON
Vice President, Children's and Family Programs

DAVID WEDECK
Vice President, Programs, East Coast

WINIFRED WHITE
Vice President, Family Programs

AMY ADELSON
Director, Mini-series and Novels for TV

PAM DAWSON
Director, Game Programs

JANET FAUST KRUSI
Director, Motion Pictures for TV

DAN FILLE
Director, Drama Programs

JAY RODRIGUEZ
Vice President, Corporate Information

TOM GABBAY
Director, Children's Programs

PATTI GRANT
Director, Late Night Prgrams

DAVID A. NEUMAN
Director, Current Comedy Programs

BRIAN PIKE
Director, Motion Pictures for TV

RUTH SLAWSON
Director, Motion Pictures for TV

KEN RASKOFF
Director, Motion Pictures for TV

DONNA SWAJESKI
Director, Daytime Drama, East Coast

DEAN VALENTINE
Director, Comedy Development

JOHN AGOGLIA
Executive Vice President, Business Affairs

LAYNE L. BRITTON
Vice President, Program & Talent Negotiations

JOSEPH BURES
Vice President, Program Acquisitions

BUD RUKEYSER, JR.
Executive Vice President, Corporate Communications

JAY MICHELIS
Vice President, Corporate and Media Relations, West Coast

PAY, CABLE
& TELECOMMUNICATION
COMPANIES

ARTS & ENTERTAINMENT NETWORK
555 Fifth Avenue
New York, NY 10017
Tel: (212) 661-4500
Tel.: (213) 933-7496 (West Coast)

Nicholas Davatzes-President & Chief
  Executive Officer
Peter Hansen-Vice President,
  Programs
Betty Cornfeld-Director of Programs
Pat Kehoe-Marketing
Matt Tombers-West coast

THE DISNEY CHANNEL
3800 W. Alameda Ave.
Burbank, CA 91521
Tel.: (818) 840-1000

John F. Cooke - President
Patrick Davidson - Vice President
Paulo de Oliveira - Vice President -
Program Development
Tom Epstein - Vice President - Public
Relations
Stephen D. Fields - Vice President -
Marketing
Mark Handler - Vice President - Sales
and Affiliate Relations
Patrick Lopker - Vice President -
Finance & Treasurer
Michael O'Gara - Vice President -
Production
Bruce Rider - Vice president - Pro-
gramming
Dean Waite - Vice president - Sales
and Affiliate Relations, East

Lynn Woodard - National Accounts
Tom Wzsalek - Vice President -
Consumer Marketing
Carol Rubin - Director of Film Devel-
opment

HOME BOX OFFICE
1100 Avenue of the Americas
New York, NY 10036
Telephone: (212) 512-1000

West coast:
2049 Century Park East
Los Angeles, CA 90067
Tel.: (213) 201-9200

Michael Fuchs- Chairman and
  Chief Executive Officer
Joe Collins-President
Seth Abraham-Sr. Vice President,
  Programming Operations & Sports
Larry Aidem-Vice President, Original
  Program Planning & Operations
Chris Albrecht-Sr. Vice President,
  Original Programming, West Coast
Don Anderson-Sr. Vice President,
  Black Entertainment Television
Dave Baldwin-Vice President,
  Program Planning
Dick Beahrs-Senior Vice President,
  Cinemax Sales & Marketing
Jeff Bewkes-Senior Vice President,
  Chief Financial Officer
Rick Bieber-Senior Vice President,
  HBO PIctures & Programming Oper.
John Billock-Sr.Vice President, Market-
ing

Betty Bitterman-Vice President,
Original Programming
Tin Braine-Vice Pres. & Exec. Pro-
ducer, On-Air Promotion
Jeff Bricmont-Vice Pres., Original
Programming, West Coast
Larry Carlson-Sr. Vice Pres., Cinemax
& New Business Development
Lucy Chudson-Vice President,
Family Programming
Horace Collins-Sr. Vice Pres., Chief
Counsel, Film Programming
Lee deBoer-Sr. Vice pres., Cinemax &
Program Planning
Pat Fili-Vice President, Business
Affairs & Production
Shelley Fischel-Sr. Vice President,
Human Resources
Cathy Fitzpatrick-Vice President,
Production, West Coast
Peter Frame-Exec. Vice President,
Affiliate Sales & Operations
Bob Grassi-Sr. Vice Pres., Sales
Operations & Administration
Ross Greenberg-Vice Pres. & Executive
Producer, HBO Sports
Bob Greenway-Vice pres.,
Sports Programming
Tom Hammel-Vice President,
Production, HBO Pictures
Bill Hooks-Sr. Vice Pres.,
Affiliate Operations
Ilene Kahn-Vice President,
HBO Pictures
Henry Mc Gee-Vice President,
Home Video
Sheila Nevins-Vice President,
Documentaries & Family Programs
John Newton-Vice President,
Film Programming
Neil Pennella-Vice President, Business
Affairs & Film Acquisition

Bridget Potter-Sr. Vice President,
Original Programming
David B. Pritchard-Vice President,
Corporate Affairs
John Redpath-Sr. Vice President,
General Counsel
Bill Sanders-Vice President, Original
Programming-West Coast
Quentin Schaffer-V.P. Media Relations
Steve Scheffer-Exec. Vice President,
Film Programming & Home Video
Henry Schleiff-Sr. Vice President,
Business Affairs & Administration
Stu Smiley-Vice President, Comedy
East Coast
Stan Thomas Sr. Vice President,
Affiliate Operations
Steve Ujlaki-Vice President,
HBO Pictures
Jim Warner-Vice President
HBO Enterprises
Glenn Whitehead-Vice President,
Business Affairs, West Coast

MTV NETWORKS
(a subsidiary of Viacom, Inc.)
10 Universal City Plaza
Universal City, CA 91608
Tel.: (818) 505-7500

Tom E. Freston-President & Chief
Executive Officer, MTV
Networks Entertainment
Geraldine B. Laybourne-Executive
Vice Pres. & General Manager,
Nickelodeon and Nick at Nite
John Reardon-Executive Vice Pres.
and General Manager Affiliate
Sales and Marketing

MTV NETWORKS continued

Lee Masters-Senior Vice Pres. and
General Manager MTV: Music Tele-
vision & VH-1/Video Hits One
Debby Beece-Vice Pres., Programming,
Nickelodeon & Nick at Nite
Geoffrey Darby-Vice President,
Production
Nickelodeon & Nick at Nite
Juli Davidson-Vice Pres. amd Creative
Supervisor, Creative Services
Anthony C. Fiore-Vice Pres., Eastern
Sales Manager MTV & VH-1
Doug Herzog-Vice Pres., News and
Special Programming/MTV
Linda M. Kahn-Vice pres., Acquisi-
tions,
Nickelodeon & Nick at Nite
Samuel M. Kaiser-Vice President,
Music Programming, MTV
Judith McGrath-Vice President &
Creative Director, MTV
Jeffrey A. Rowe-Vice President,
VH-1/Video Hits One

SHOWTIME/THE MOVIE CHAN-
NEL
10 Universal City Plaza. 31st Floor
Universal City, CA 91608
Tel.: (818) 505-7500

Fred Schneier-Executiv eVice Presi-
dent, Programming
Jack Heim-Executive Vice President,
Business Development Sales &
Affiliate Marketing

John Burns-Senior Vice President,
Affiliate Sales & Marketing
Jim Miller-Senior Vice President of
Program Acquisitions & Planning
Josh Sapan-Senior Vice Pres., Market-
ing and Creative Services
Dennis L. Balthazor-Vice President,
Western Region
C. David Batalsky-Vice President,
Special Events
Barbara Bellafiore-Vice President,
Sales Strategy
Richard Bencivengo-Vice President,
Production
Howard Bryks—Vice President,
Business Information Services
Howard Crotin-Vice President,
Sales Administration
Mathew Duda-Vice President,
Program Planning
Tom Furr-Vice President,
Program Promotion
Stu Ginsberg-Vice President , Press
And Public Relations
Barry Goldberg-Vice President,
Southeast Region
Art Gusow-Regional Vice President,
Northeast
Bruce Heller-Vice President,
Business Affairs
Steve Hewitt-Vice President, Original
Programming, East Coast
Rick Howe-Vice President,
Affiliate Marketing
Dick Ingebrand-Vice President
North Central Region
Dennis Johnson-Vice President,
Original Programming, West Coast
Gary Keeper-Vice President,
Original Programming
Michael Klein-Vice President,
Film Acquisitions

McAdory Lipscomb, Jr.-Vice President,
Rocky Mountain Region
Ann Foley Plunkett-Vice President,
Creative Services
Gwen Marcus-Vice President, Counsel
George Robertson-Vice President,
Market Strategy
William Rogers-Vice President,
Business Affairs
Nora Ryan-Vice President,
Marketing Operations
Natalie Seaver-Vice President,
Dramatic Development
Micahel Seeger-Vice President,
Operations
and Production Services
Andrew Sereysky-Vice President,
Advertising
Jim Shaw-Vice President, Financial
Planning & Bus. Administration
Alan Zapakin-Vice President,
Scheduling

USA NETWORK
1230 Avenue of the Americas
New York, NY 10020
Tel.: (212) 408-9100

Kay Koplovitz-President and
Chief Executive Officer
R. Kent Replogle-Executive V.P.,
Chief Operating Officer
David Bender-V.P., Research
Andrew Besch-V.P., Marketing
Stephen Brenner-V.P., Business
Affairs & General Counsel
Douglas Hamilton-V.P., Finance
and Aministration
Gil Faccio-Senior V.P.,
Affiliate Relations
David Klein-Senior V.P.,
Programming
John Silvestri-Senior V.P.,
Advertising Sales
Susan Schulman-Director,
Public Relations

**TWENTIETH CENTURY FOX
VIDEO AND PAY TELEVISION**
10201 W. Pico Blvd.
Los Angeles, CA 90035
Tel.: (213) 277-2211

Robert M. Kreek-Executive Vice
President,
Fox, Inc. & Senior Vice Pres., Home
Video
and Pay Television
George Krieger-Vice President,
Pay Television Sales
Sam Weinstein-Vice President,
Worldwide Non-theatrical Sales
Michael Binkow-Vice President,
Corporate Communications, Fox, Inc.

Academy of Television Arts & Sciences
1988 Officers and Executives

Doug Duitsman
President

Leo Chaloukian
First Vice President

Jan Scott
Second Vice President

John Furia
Secretary

Richard Frank
Imediate Past President

Jay Strong
Los Angeles Area
Vice President

Mel Sawelson
Treasurer

James L. Loper
Academy Executive Director

AGENTS and AGENCIES

The following rosters of agents that are listed below represent many of the writers, directors, and producers found in the book

THE AGENCY
10351 Santa Monica Blvd.
Suite 211
Los Angeles, CA 90025
Tel.: (213) 551-3000

Jerome Zeitman
Laurence Becsey
Richard C, Berman
Scott Henderson
Frank Wuligar
Fred Engel
Jodi Levine
Marti Blumenthal

**AGENCY FOR THE
PERFORMING ARTS (APA)**
9000 Sunset Boulevard, 12th Fl.
Los Angeles, CA 90069
Tel.: (213) 273-0744

John Gaines
Marty Klein
Tom Korman
Peter Giagni
Geoff Brandt
Ina Bernstein

BAUER-BENEDEK AGENCY
9255 Sunset Boulevard, Suite 716
Los Angeles, CA 90069
Tel.: (213) 275-2421

Martin Bauer
Peter Benedek

**BRODER/KURLAND/WEBB
AGENCY**
8439 Sunset Boulevard, Suite 402
Los Angeles, CA 90069
Tel.: (213) 656-9262

Bob Broder
Normand Kurland
Elliott Webb

CONTEMPORARY ARTISTS LTD.
132 S. Lasky Drive
Beverly Hills, CA 90212
Tel.: (213) 278-8250

Ronnie Lief
Al Melnick
Richard Lewis

THE COOPER AGENCY
10100 Santa Monica Blvd., #310
Los Angeles, CA 90067
Tel.: (213) 277-8422

Frank Cooper
Jeff Cooper

CREATIVE ARTISTS AGENCY (CAA)
1888 Century Park East, Suite 1400
Los Angeles, CA 90067
Tel.: (213) 277-4545

Michael Ovitz
Mike Marcus
Martin Baum
Robert Bookman
Ron Meyer
Rowland Perkins
Bob Graham
David Greenblatt
Rand Holston
Tony Ludwig
Tina Nides
Cheryl Peterson
Jack Rapke
Mike Rosenfeld
Rosalie Swedlin
Paula Wagner

INTERNATIONAL CREATIVE MANAGEMENT (ICM)
8899 Bevery Boulevard
Los Angeles, CA 90048
Tel.: (213) 550-4000

Jeff Berg
Ben Benjamin
Bill Bloch
Sam Cohn (New York)
Arlene Donovan (New York)
Martha Luttrell
David Lonner
Michael Oliver
Lou Pitt
Bill Robinson
Allen Sabinson
Paul Schwartzman
Jane Sindell
Jim Wiatt
Jeremy Zimmer

LEADING ARTISTS, INC
445 North Bedford Dr.
Penthouse
Beverly Hills, CA 90210
Tel.: (213) 858-1999

Robert Stein
James Berkus
Gary Cosay
Sue Cameron
Robb Rothman
Patricia Hacker
Toby Jaffe
Virginia Giritlian
Ann Dollard
Bruce Tufeld

WILLIAM MORRIS AGENCY

151 El Camino Drive
Beverly Hills, CA 90212
Tel.: (213) 274-7451

Lee Stevens
Roger Davis
Leonard Hirshan
Boaty Boatwright
John Burnham
Anthony Frantozzi
Tony Howard
Joan Hyler
Ed Limato
Ron Mardigan
Michael Peretzian
John Ptak
Judy Scott-Fox
Peter Turner
Carol Yumkas

TRIAD ARTISTS

10100 Santa Monica Boulevard
16th Floor
Los Angeles, CA 90067
Tel.: (213) 56-2727

Sam Adams
Rick Ray
Richard rosenberg
Arnold Rifkin
John Kimble
Gene Parseghian
Peter Grosslight
Richard Rosenberg

SHAPIRO-LICHTMAN

8827 Beverly Boulevard
Los Angeles, CA 90048
Tel.: (213) 859-8877

Martin Shapiro
Mark Lichtman

INDEX TO COMPANIES

144

INDEX
to
INDIVIDUALS

NOTES

NOTES

Update & Ordering Information

If you or your company need additional copies of **WHO'S WHO IN TELEVISION**, please use the form below.

Parkard Communications prepares an update supplement to **WHO'S WHO** between editions. This will notify you of important changes in the books, such as new addresses, new listings, company roster updates, and other additional information. The aim is to keep your book as current as possible as the industry changes.

To receive an announcement of the next edition of WHO'S WHO, check the box below.

Return to: PACKARD HOUSE BOOKS
                    P.O. BOX 2187
                    Beverly Hills, Calif. 90213

Please send me_____ copy (ies) of WHO'S WHO IN TELEVISION at $18.95 @ plus $1.25 for shipping in the U.S. (Canada, $2.75). For all other countries add $4.75 (via Air). California residents please add $1.19.

☐ **Please send me a Mid-Edition Update at $2.00 each, (Available Feb. 1988)**
☐ **Mail me an announcement for the next edition**

_____
name

_____
Company

_____
address

_____

.....coming soon

WHO'S WHO
IN THE MOTION
PICTURE
INDUSTRY

6TH Edition